FLAG FOOTBALL
6v6
PLAYBOOK

Jordon Replogle

FLAG FOOTBALL 6v6 PLAYBOOK

Jordon Replogle

Published by Jordon Replogle, 2024.

While every precaution has been taken in the preparation of this book, the publisher assumes no responsibility for errors or omissions, or for damages resulting from the use of the information contained herein.

FLAG FOOTBALL 6V6 PLAYBOOK

First edition. February 12, 2024.

ISBN: 979-8224599998

Written by Jordon Replogle.

FLAG FOOTBALL 6v6 PLAYBOOK

Intro

Dive into the strategic world of flag football with Jordon Replogle, a seasoned gridiron veteran with a passion for the game that spans playing fields and coaching sidelines alike. In this comprehensive playbook, Replogle shares his wealth of experience, providing readers with a tactical roadmap to elevate their flag football game.

"Flag Football 6v6 Playbook" is not just a guide; it's a treasure trove of insider knowledge derived from Replogle's remarkable journey through high school, college, semi-pro, and arena football. As a coach with eight seasons of flag football under his belt, Jordon seamlessly translates his on-field prowess into a resource that caters to players and coaches at all levels.

Inside this playbook, readers will find a dynamic array of sample plays that have been battle-tested on the field. From clever offensive formations to strategic defensive setups. The book also features a sample practice outline, allowing coaches to structure their training sessions effectively, maximizing player development and team cohesion.

One unique highlight of the playbook is the inclusion of play sheets and wristband plays, providing practical tools for immediate implementation on the field. Replogle's meticulous attention to detail ensures that both novice and experienced players can grasp the intricacies of flag football strategy.

Whether you're a player looking to up your game or a coach aiming to refine your team's approach, "Flag Football 6v6 Playbook" by Jordon Replogle is your indispensable guide to mastering the art of flag football. Get ready to take your plays, formations, and overall understanding of the game to the next level with the wisdom of a true football aficionado.

Practice Outline

I. Full-Body Warm-up: Start with 5 minutes of light aerobic exercise like jogging, or jumping jacks, to elevate the heart rate and increase blood flow to the muscles.

II. Static Stretching: Hold each static stretch for 20 seconds to 40 seconds, focusing on deep, controlled breaths.

    A. Hamstring Stretch:

        1. While standing, feet together, slowly lower head to knees, keeping keens straight.

    B. Quad Stretch:

        1. While standing, pull one foot towards your glutes, keeping the knees close together.

    C. Hip Flexor Stretch:

        1. Kneel with one knee on the ground, and the other foot forward in a lunge position to stretch the hip flexors.

    D. Groin Stretch:

        1. Sit in a butterfly position, bringing the soles of your feet together and gently pressing your knees towards the ground.

    E. Triceps Stretch:

        1. Reach your hand down the center of your back, using the opposite hand to gently push on your elbow.

    F. Shoulder Stretch:

        1. Bring your arm across your chest and use the opposite hand to gently pull it towards your body.

    G. Arm Circles:

        1. Circular motions with the arms, both forward and backward, to warm up the shoulder joints.

III. Dynamic Stretching: Perform each dynamic stretch for 30 seconds to 1 minute, focusing on controlled movements. Should be preformed for about

10-15 yards.

    A. High Knees:

        1. Jog forward while lifting the knees towards the chest to engage the hip flexors.

    B. Butt Kicks:

        1. Jog forward while kicking heels up towards the glutes to stretch the quads.

    C. Side Shuffles:

        1. Shuffle laterally emphasizing quick lateral movements.

    D. Power Skips:

        1. Lift one knee towards your chest while simultaneously driving the opposite arm forward.

        2. As you bring the knee down, explode off the ground using the standing leg and bring the opposite knee up.

        3. While in the air, switch arms and continue the skipping motion, alternating legs.

    E. Forward Lunges

        1. Stand with your feet together.

        2. Take a step forward with one leg, lowering your hips until both knees are bent at approximately 90 degrees.

        3. The back knee should hover just above the ground.

        4. Push off the front foot to return to stand and repeat on the other leg.

    F. Broad Jump:

        1. Start with your feet shoulder-width apart.

        2. Lower your body into a quarter-squat position, engaging your core and keeping your chest up.

        3. Explosively jump forward, extending your hips, knees, and ankles.

        4. Focus on covering as much horizontal distance as possible with each jump.

IV. Agility Drills:

A. Cone Drills: Set up cones in a pattern and have players navigate through them, focusing on quick changes of direction.

B. Ladder Drills: Use an agility ladder for footwork drills to enhance speed and coordination.

C. Shuttle Runs: Short sprints back and forth to simulate game-like movements.

V. Skill-Specific Warm-up:

A. Practice basic flag-pulling techniques, emphasizing proper form to reduce the risk of injury during games.

B. Quarterback and receiver warm-up: have quarterbacks and receivers practice throwing, catching, and route running to improve accuracy and hand-eye coordination.

VI. Offensive Drills:

A. Individual Skill Work:

1. Quarterbacks: Passing drills, focus on accuracy and timing.

2. Receivers: Route running, catching, and agility drills.

3. Running Backs: Ball-handling, cutting, and agility drills.

B. Position-Specific Drills:

1. Quarterbacks and Receivers: Practice specific plays, work on communication and timing.

2. Running Backs: Hand offs, route running.

C. Team Offense:

1. Execute offensive plays with the entire team.

2. Focus on proper positioning, timing, and communication.

VII. Defensive Drills:

A. Individual Skill Work:

1. Defensive Backs: Flag-pulling techniques, coverage drills, and agility work.

2. Linebackers: Reading plays, pursuit drills, and flag-

pulling.

    3. Defensive Linemen: Flag-pulling, and pursuit drills.

B. Position-Specific Drills:

    1. Defensive Backs and Linebackers: Work on zone and man-to-man coverage.

    2. Defensive Linemen: Reading run and containment drills.

C. Team Defense:

    1. Practice defensive formations and strategies as a team.

    2. Emphasize communication and teamwork.

VIII. Scrimmage

IX. Team Bonding and Review:

A. End the practice with a brief team huddle or a team-building activity.

B. Remind players of upcoming goals and areas to focus on before the next practice.

OFFENSE

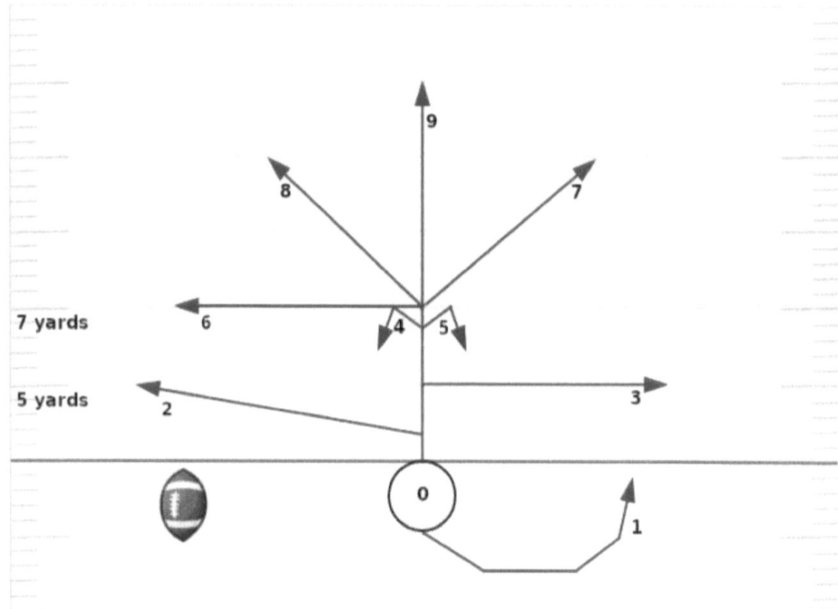

Passing Tree

0. No pattern, turn to the QB

1. Swing, short semi-circle, toward sideline

2. Slant, 2 yards, break in, toward ball at shallow angel

3. 5 yards and out, right angle, toward sideline

4. Hook, 7 yards hook in, toward ball

5. Hook, 7 yards hook out, toward sideline

6. 7 yards and in, right angle, toward ball

7. Corner, 7 yards, out, toward sideline at 45 degrees

8. Post, 7 yards, in, towards ball at 45 degrees

9. Streak or fly, run straight, look in at 7 yards

*All even numbers turn in toward ball/center, all odd numbers turn out toward sideline

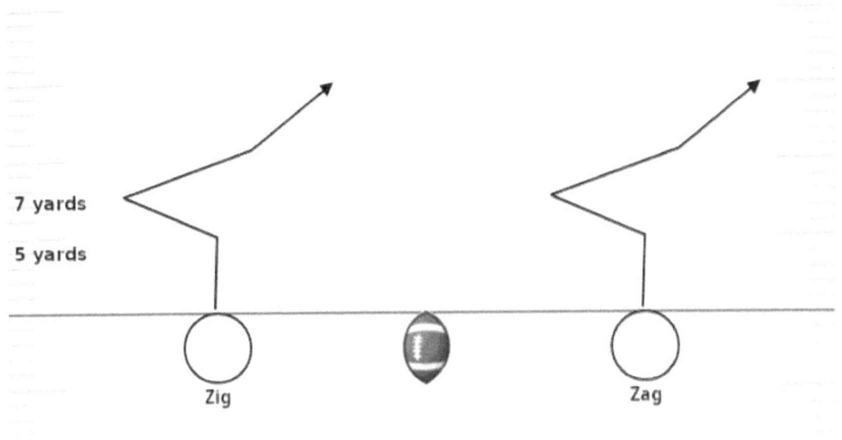

Z-Patterns

Zig – Straight 5 yards, cut toward sideline, then cut back inside

Zag – Straight 5 yards, cut toward ball, then cut back outside

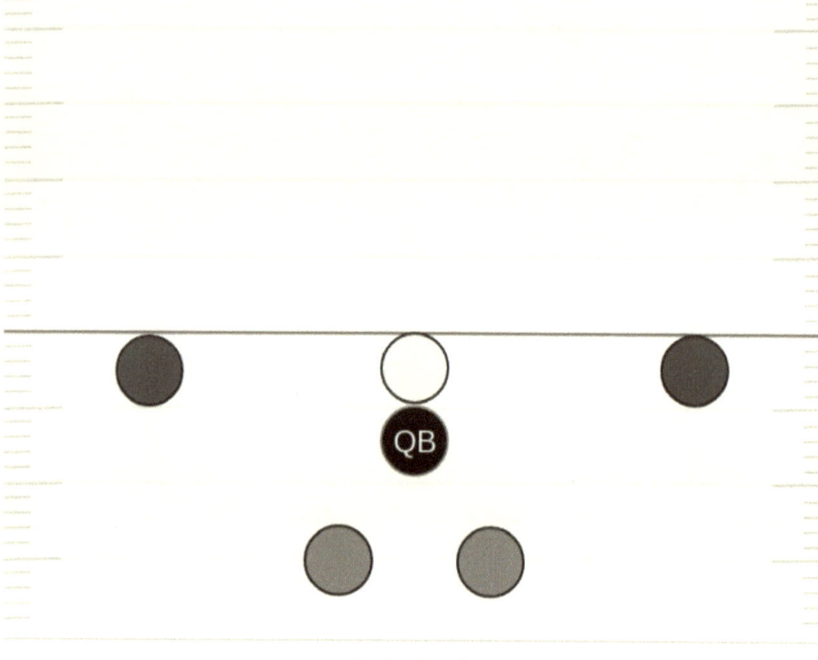

Split Backs

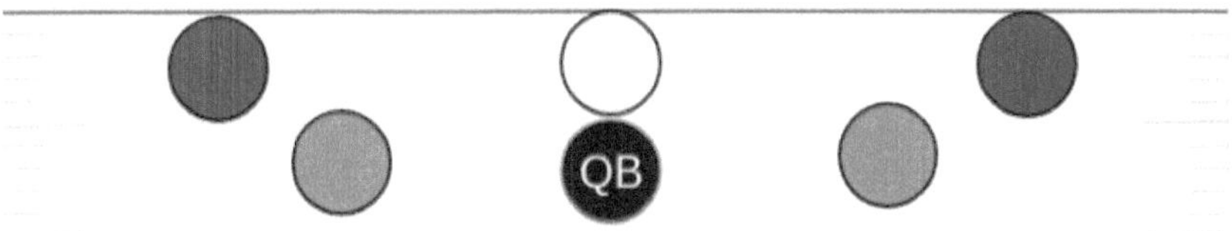

Quads

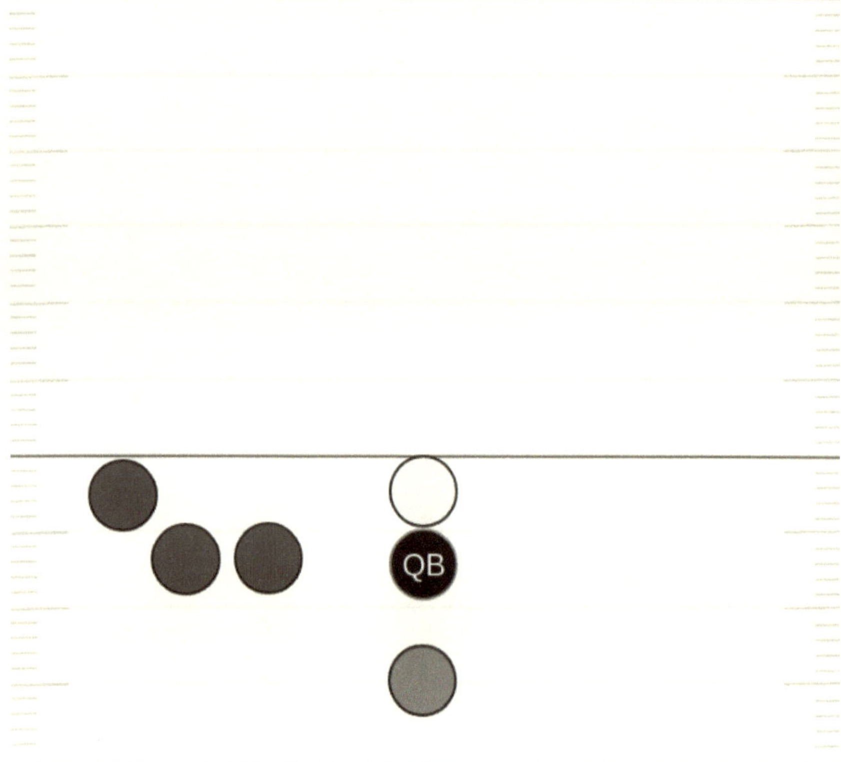

Trips Left

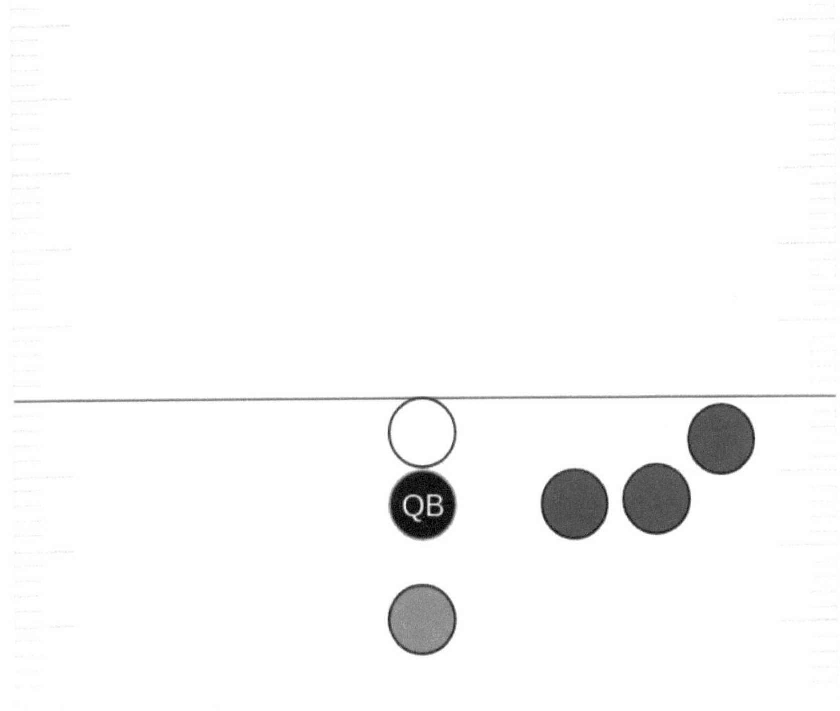

Trips Right

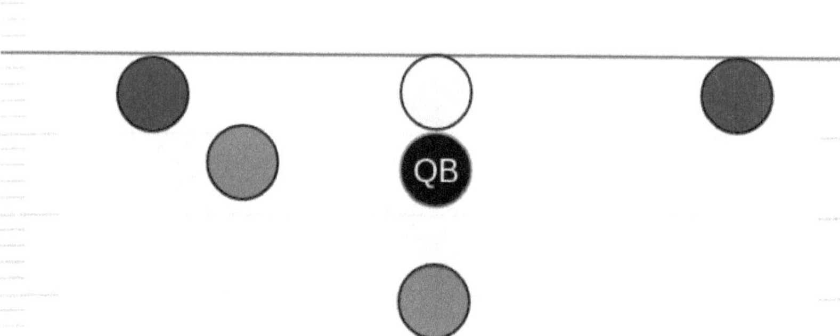

Twins Left

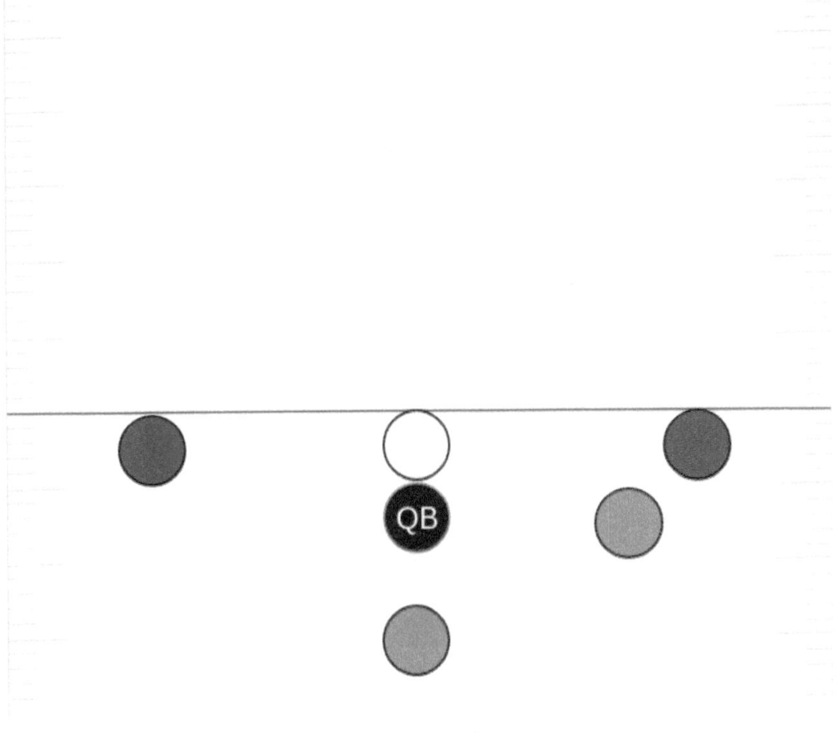

Twins Right

"Zoom"

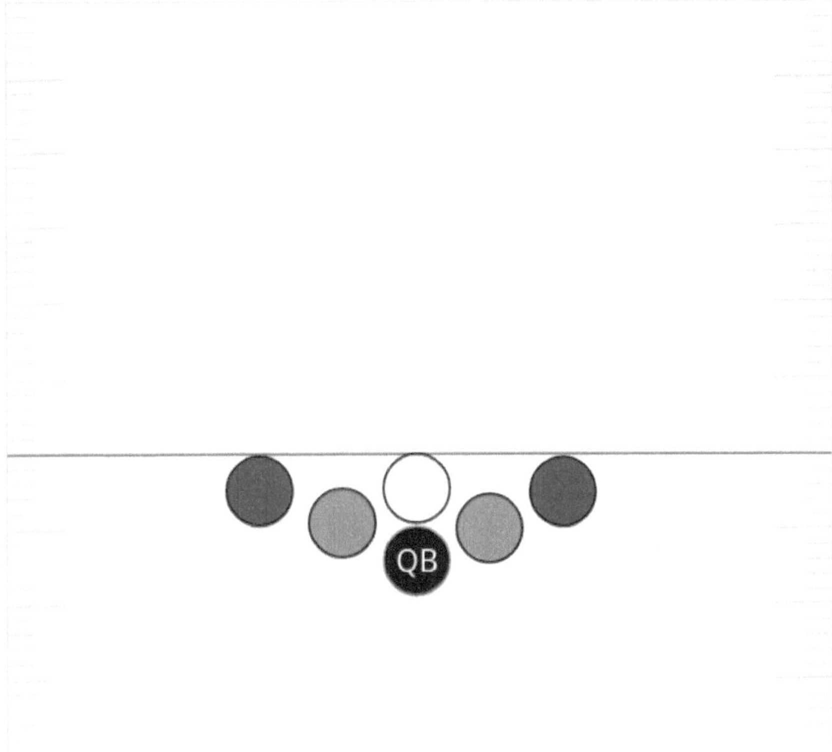

Tight

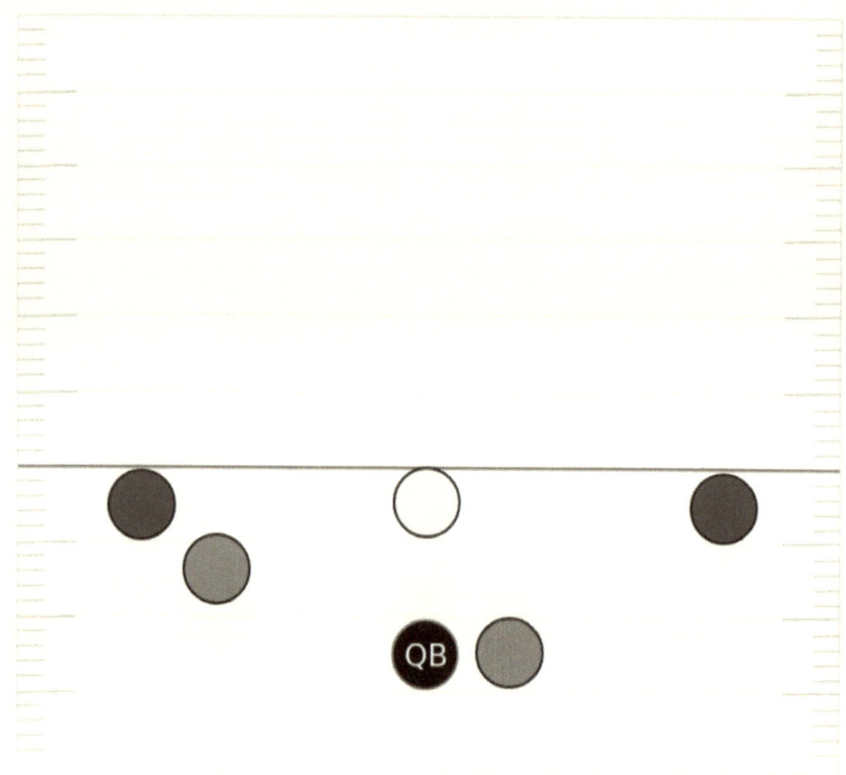

Gun Left

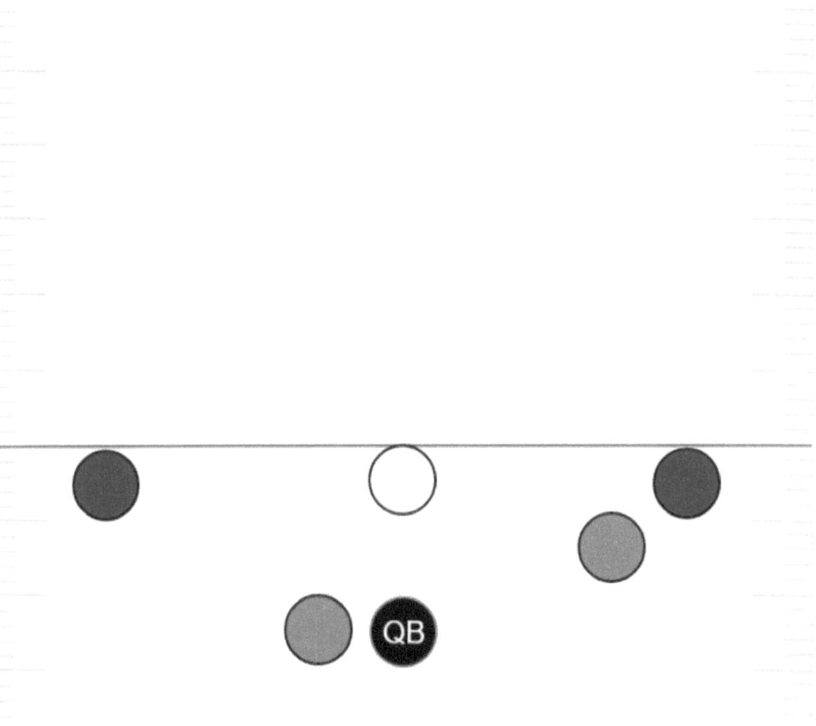

Gun Right

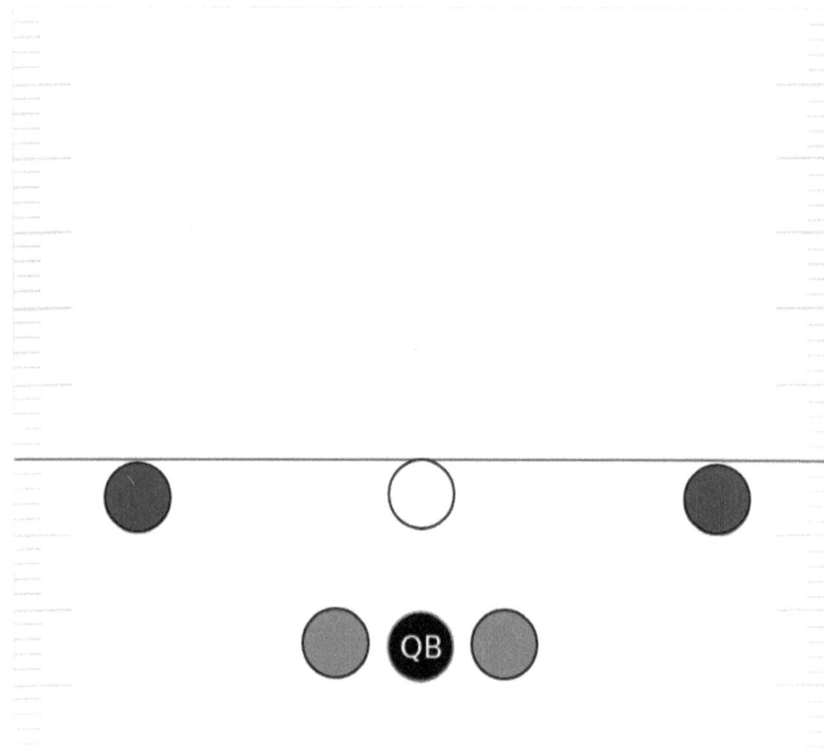

Gun Split Backs

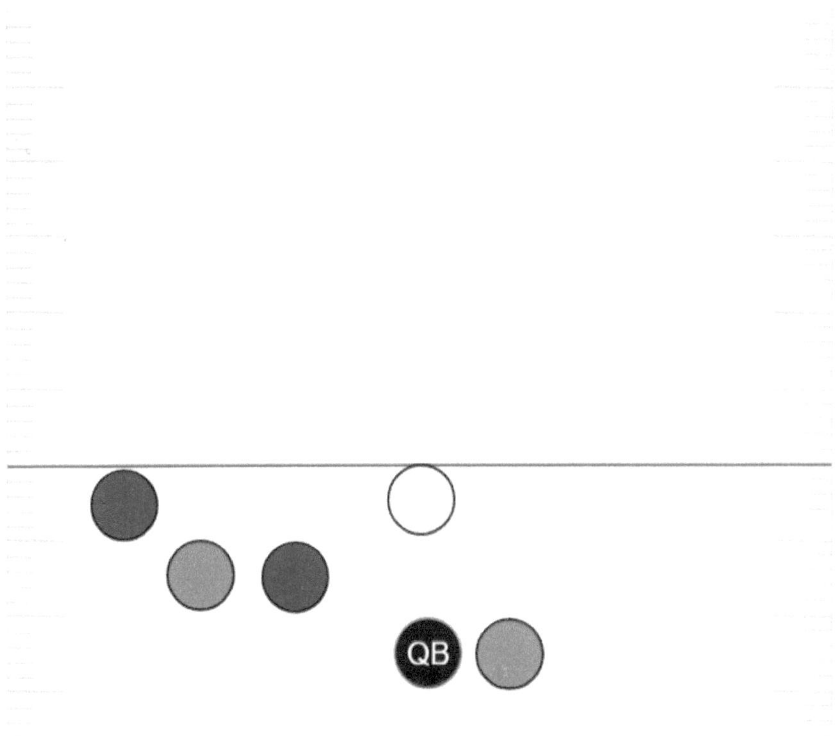

Gun Trips Left

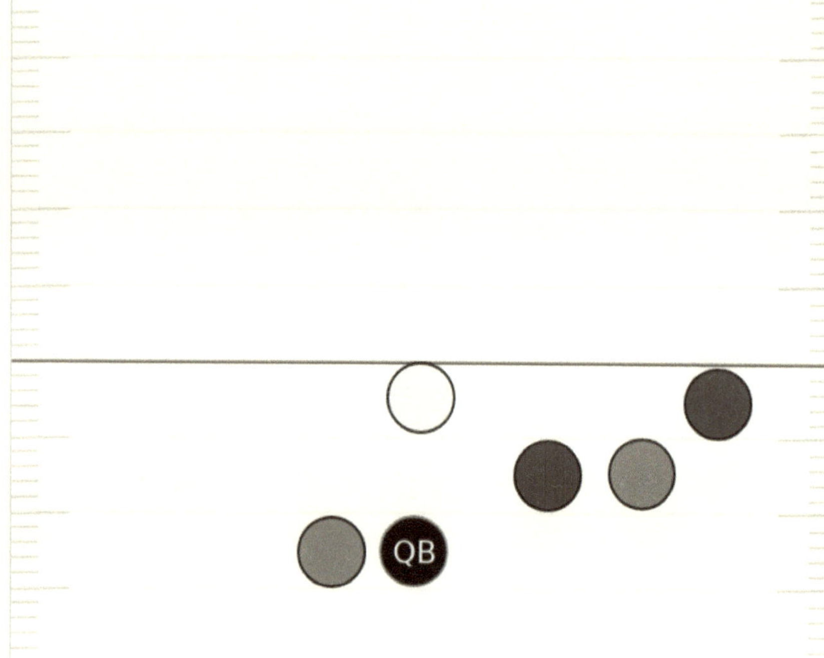

Gun Trips Right

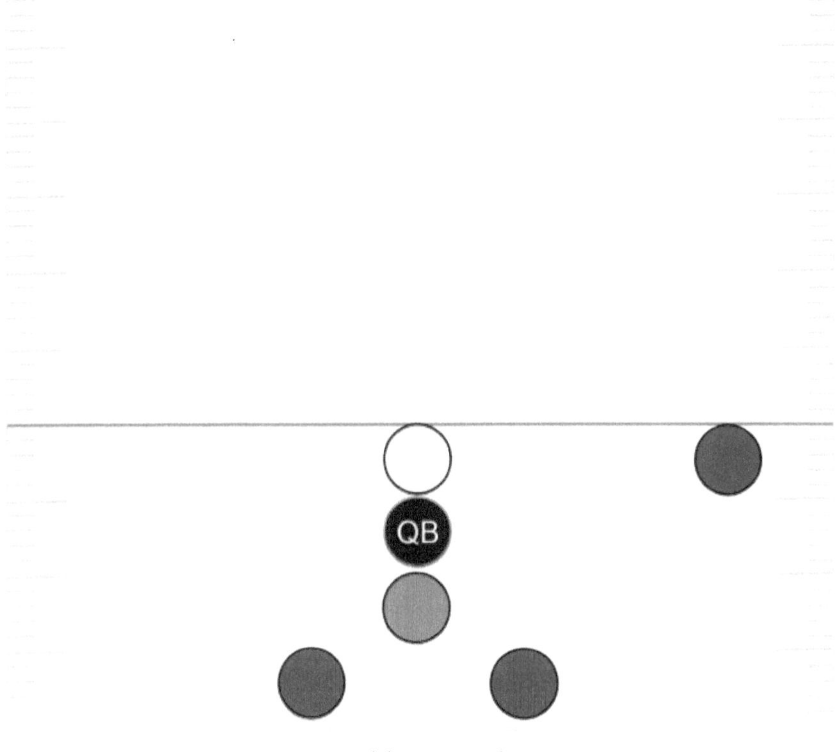

Wishbone Right

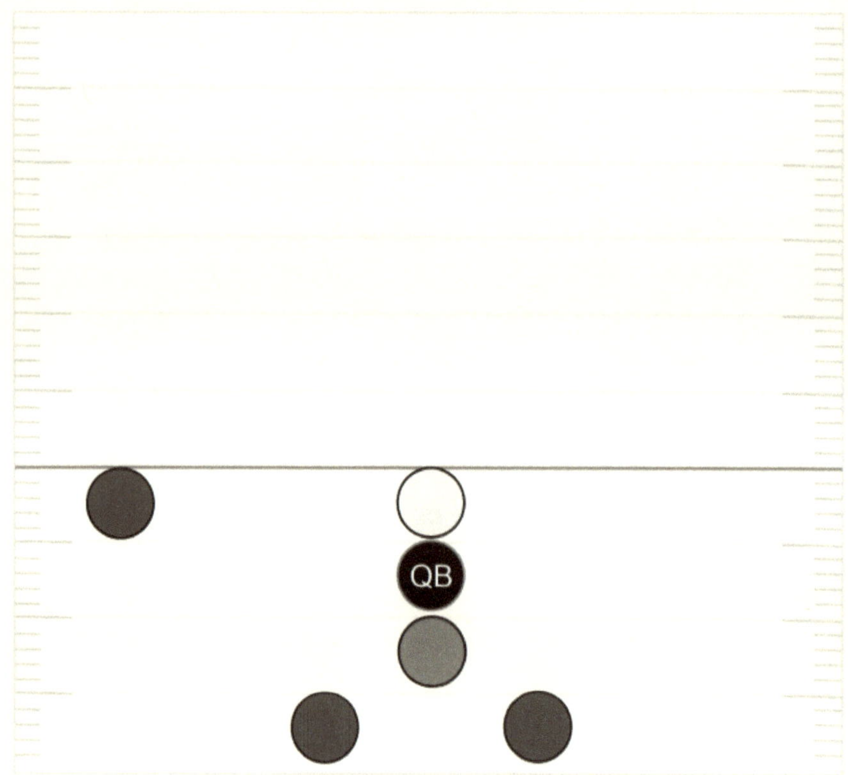

Wishbone Left

RUN PLAYS

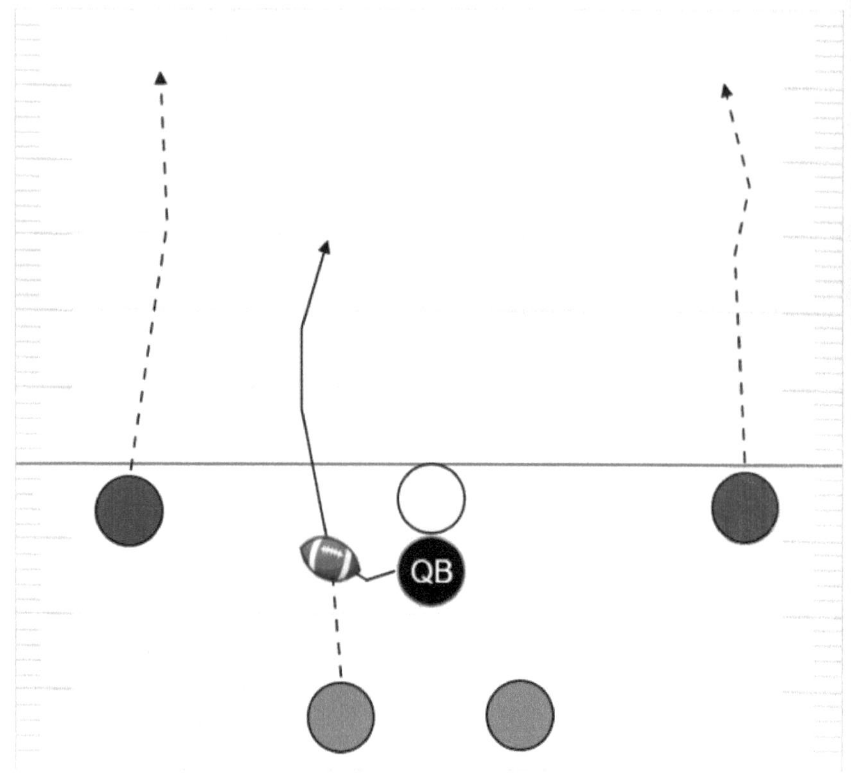

Split Backs, Dive Left

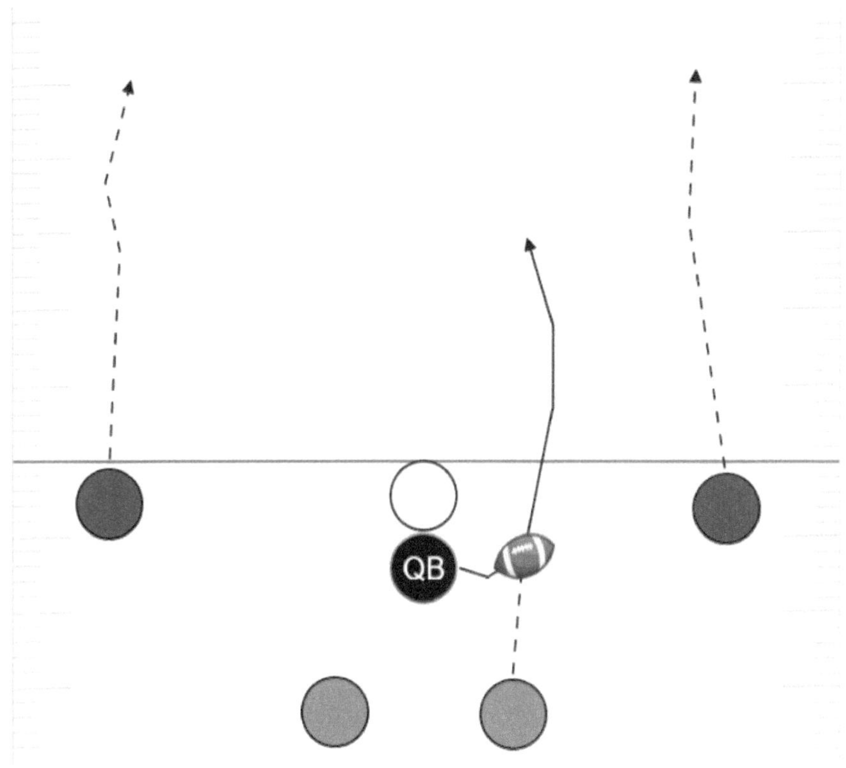

Split Backs, Dive Right

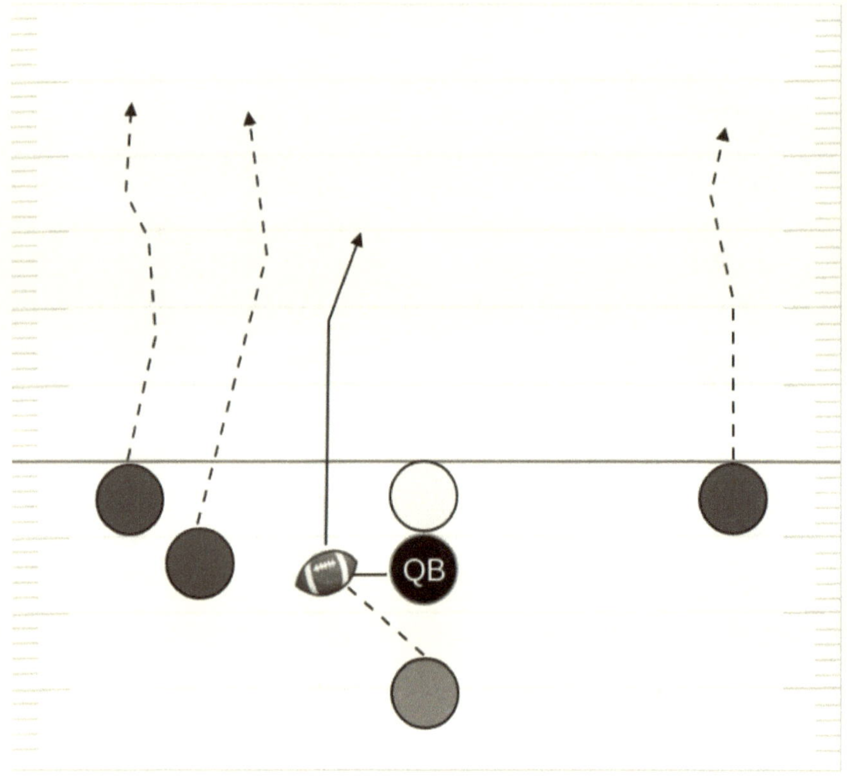

Twins Left, Dive Left

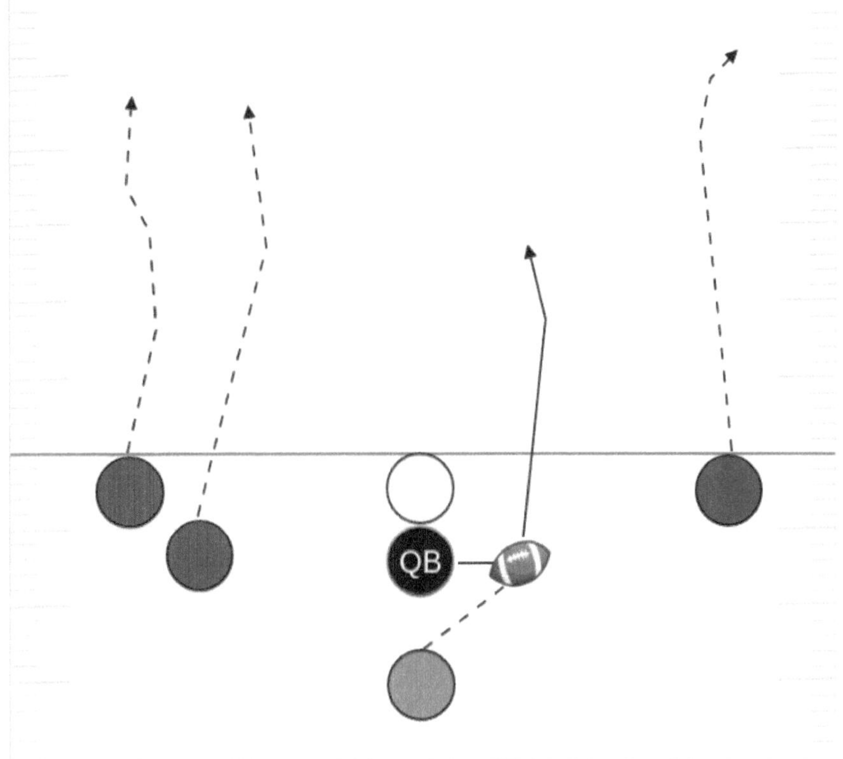

Twins Left, Dive Right

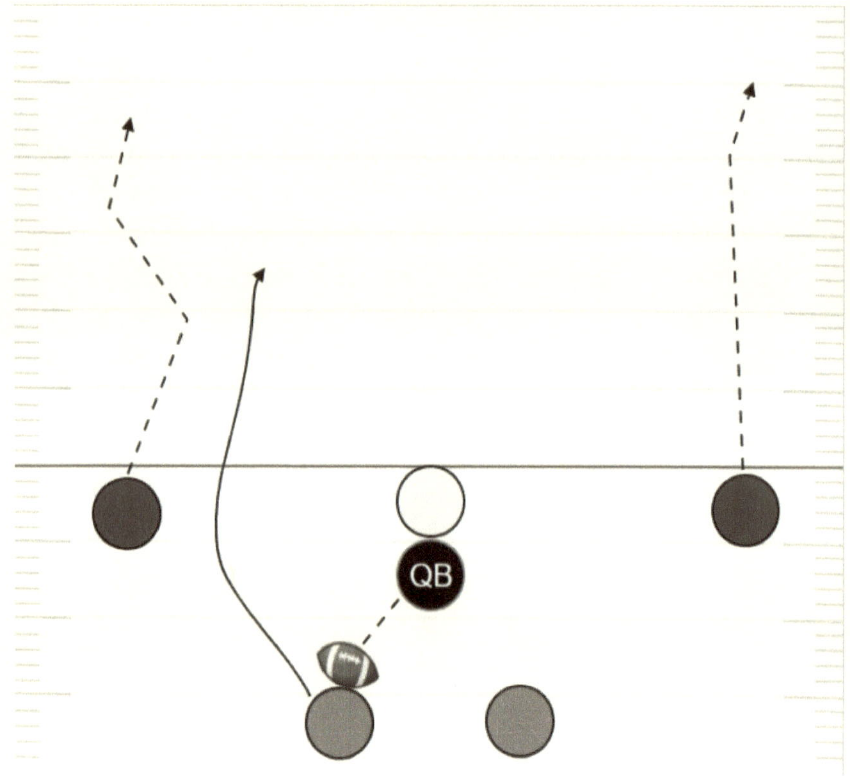

Split Backs, Pitch Left

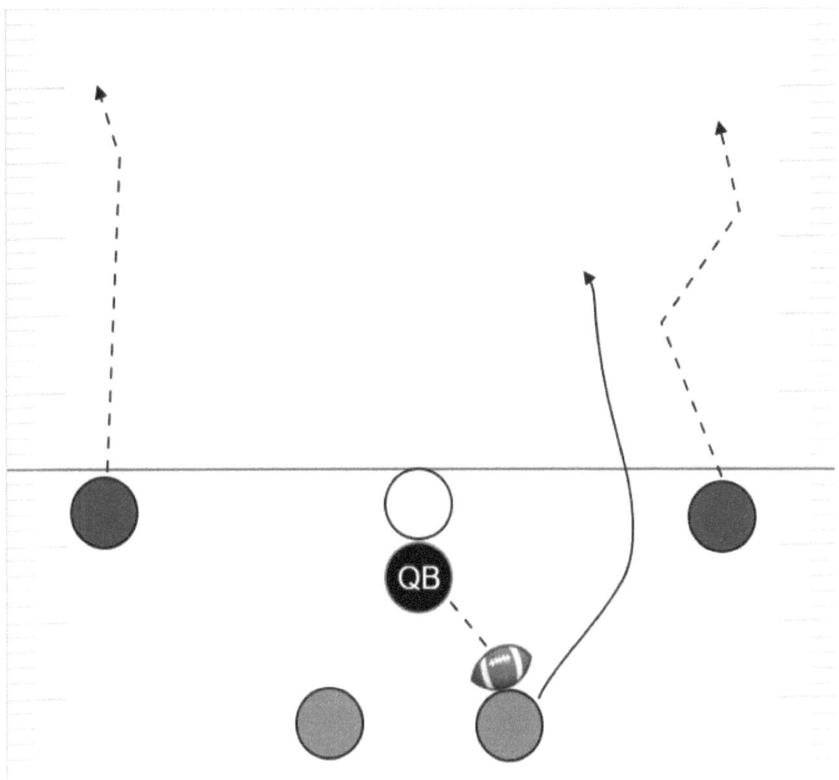

Split Backs, Pitch Right

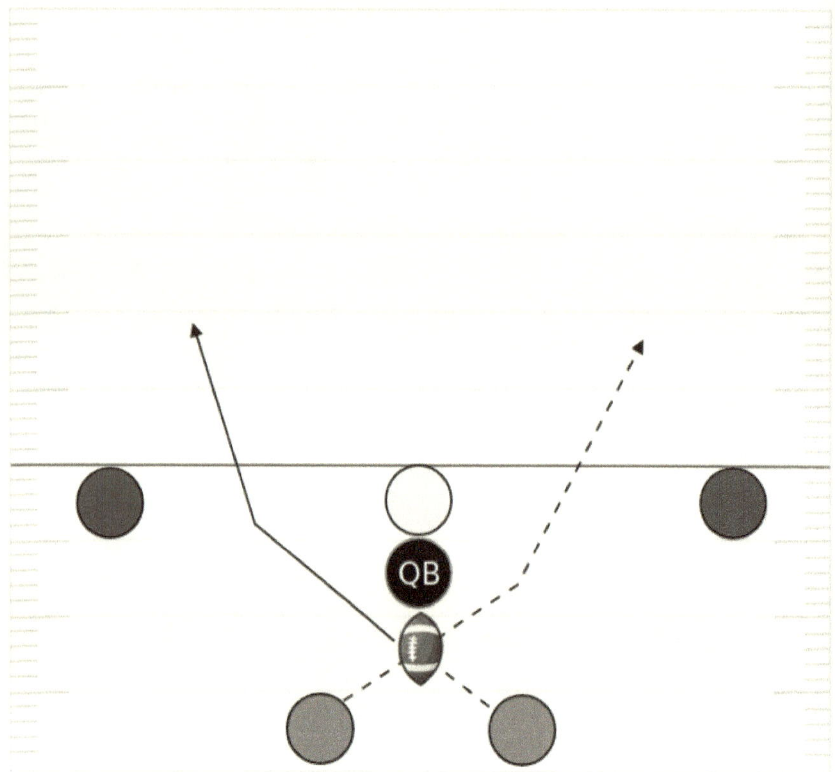

Split Backs, Cross Left
Left back moves first, faking receiving the ball
Right back goes second, taking the hand off

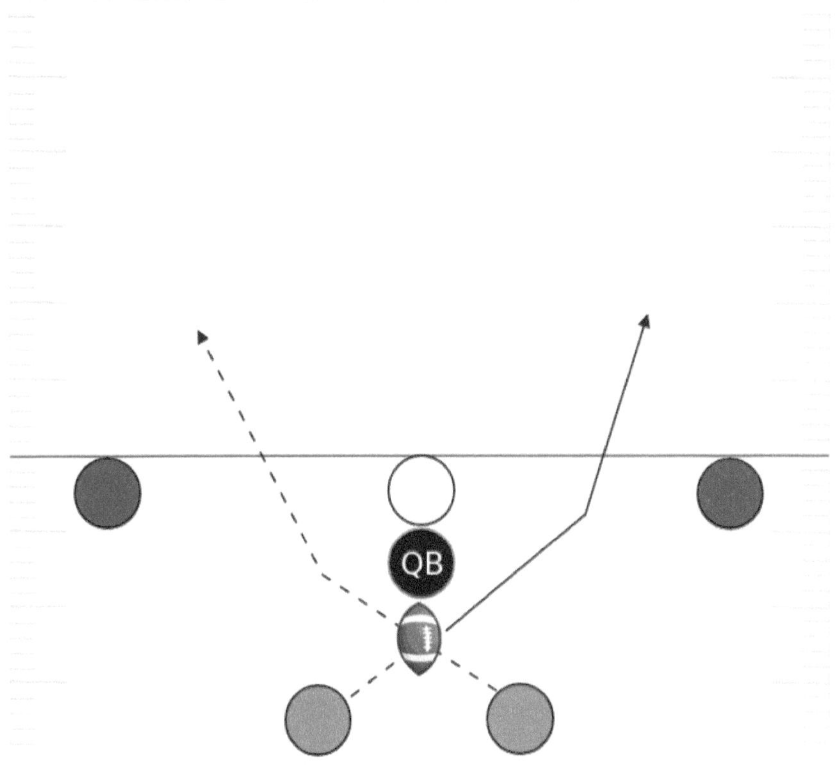

Split Backs, Cross Right
Right back moves first, faking receiving the ball
Left back goes second, taking the hand off

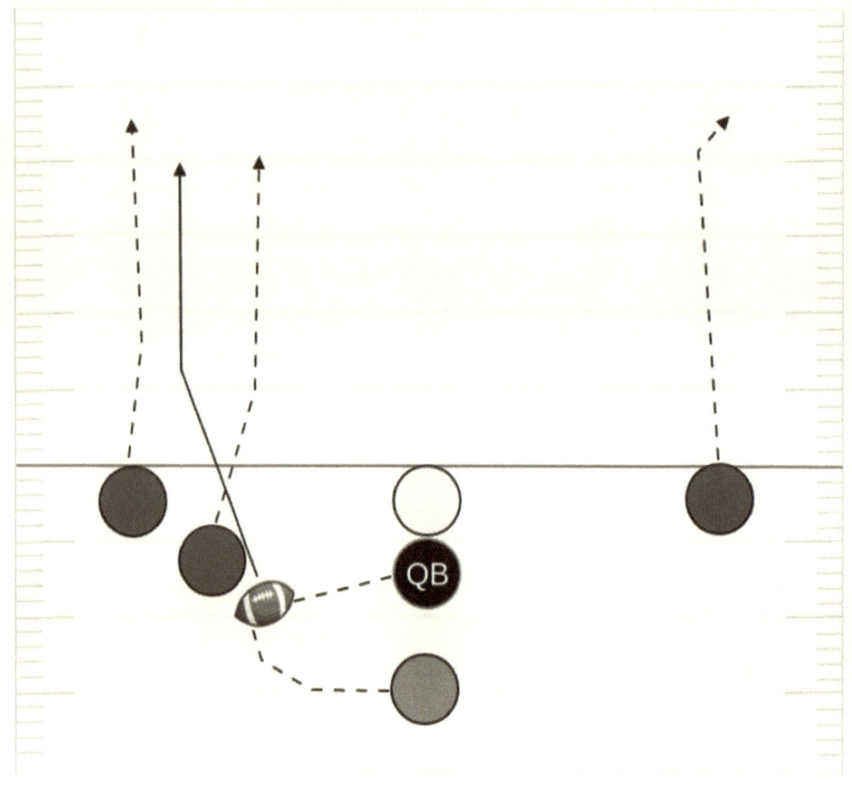

Twins Left, Pitch Left

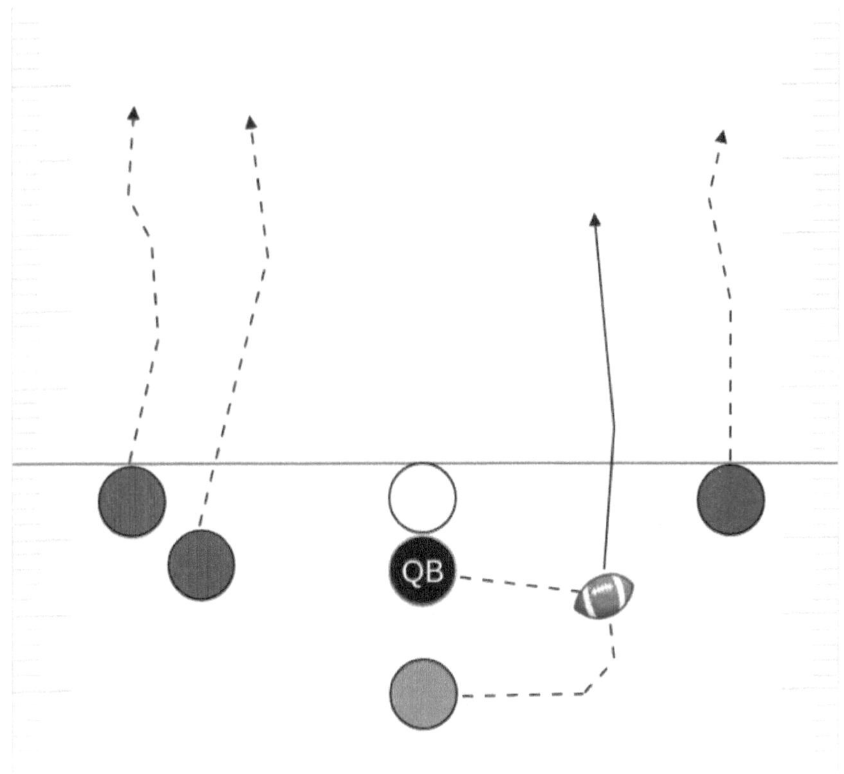

Twins Left, Pitch Right

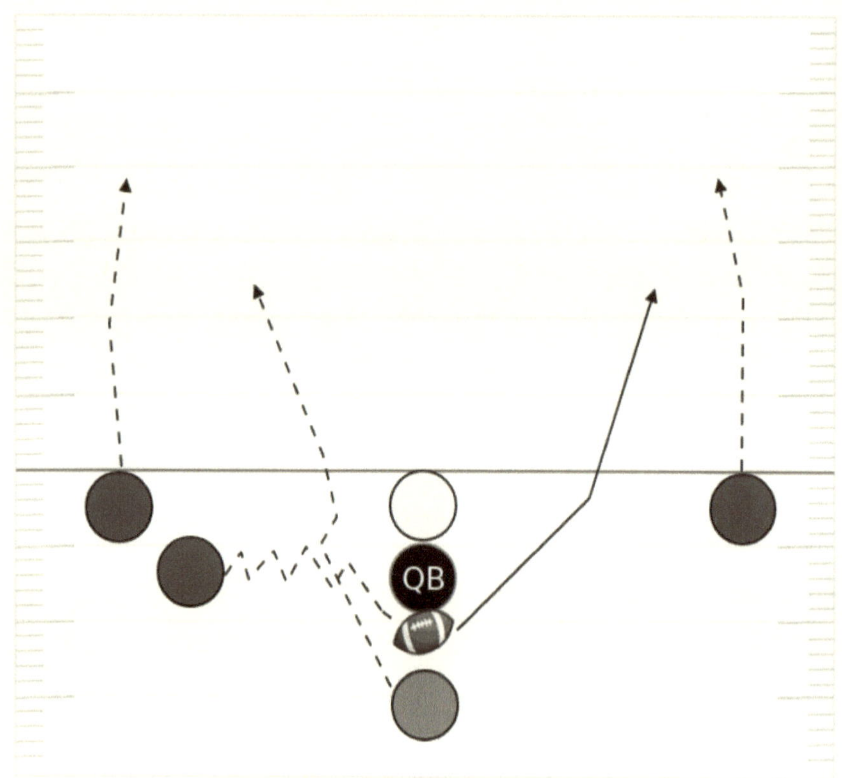

Twins Left, Jet Sweep
Slot receiver motions toward QB
QB hands off ball to slot receiver
Running back fakes left

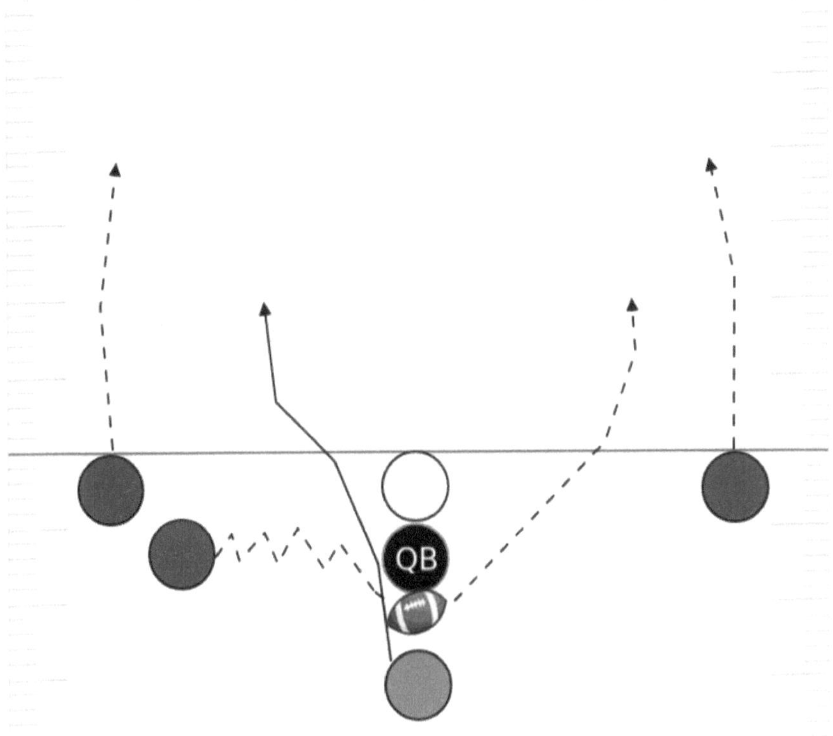

Twins Left, Jet Sweep Counter
Slot receiver motions toward QB
QB fakes hand off to slot receiver
Running back goes left, receives hand off

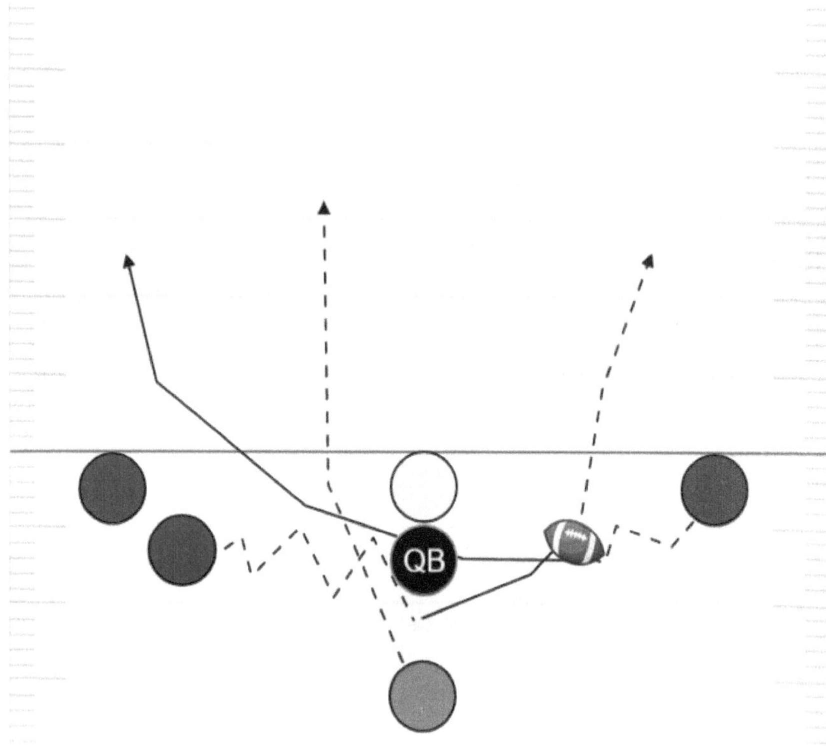

Twins Left, Jet Sweep Reverse
Slot receiver motions toward QB
QB hand off to slot receiver
Running back fakes left
Slot receiver hands off to right receiver

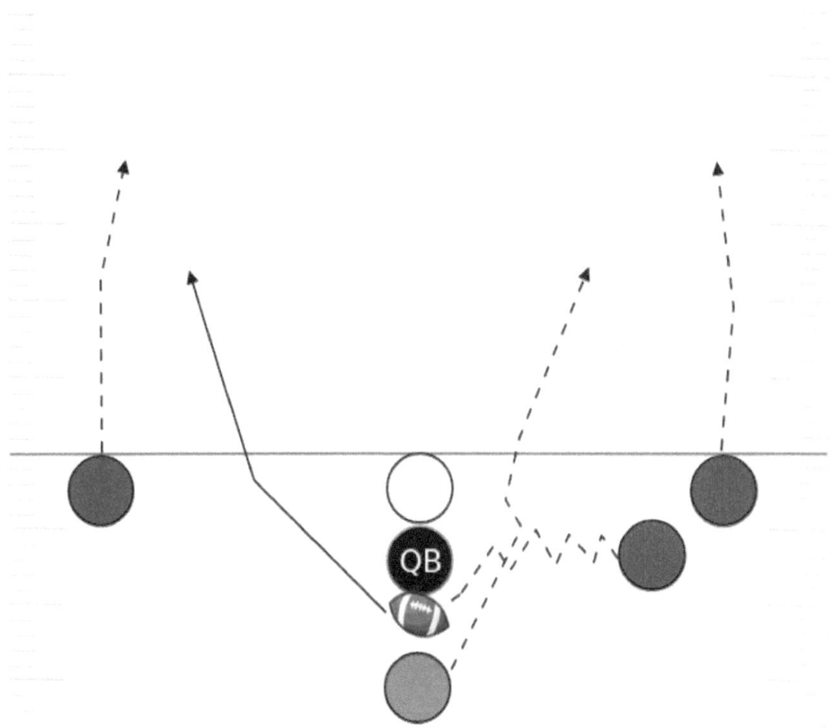

Twins Right, Jet Sweep
Slot receiver motions toward QB
QB hands off ball to slot receiver
Running back fakes right

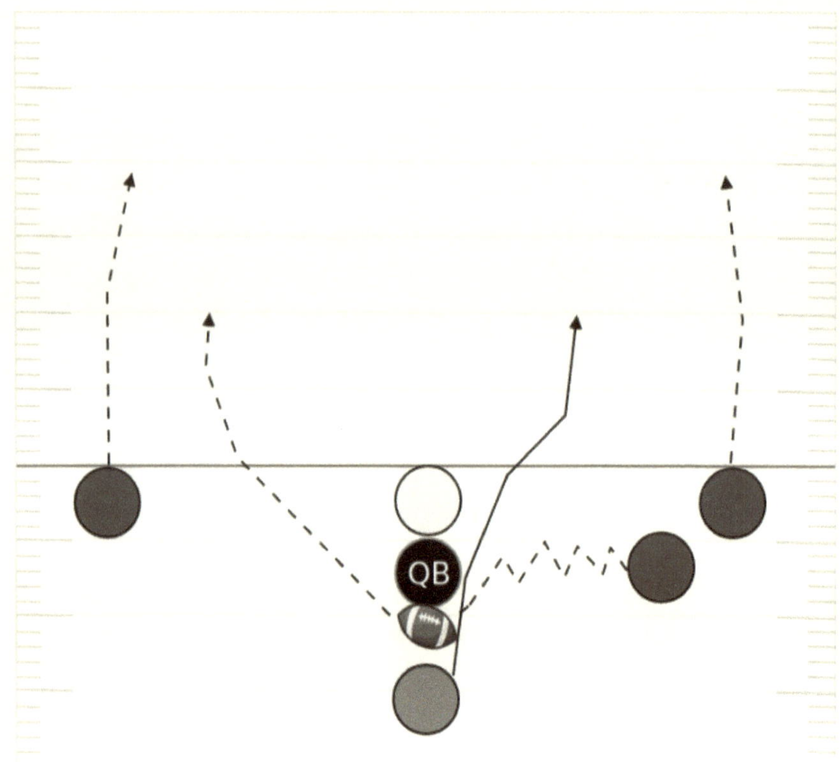

Twins Right, Jet Sweep Counter
Slot receiver motions toward QB
QB fakes hand off to slot receiver
Running back goes right, receives hand off

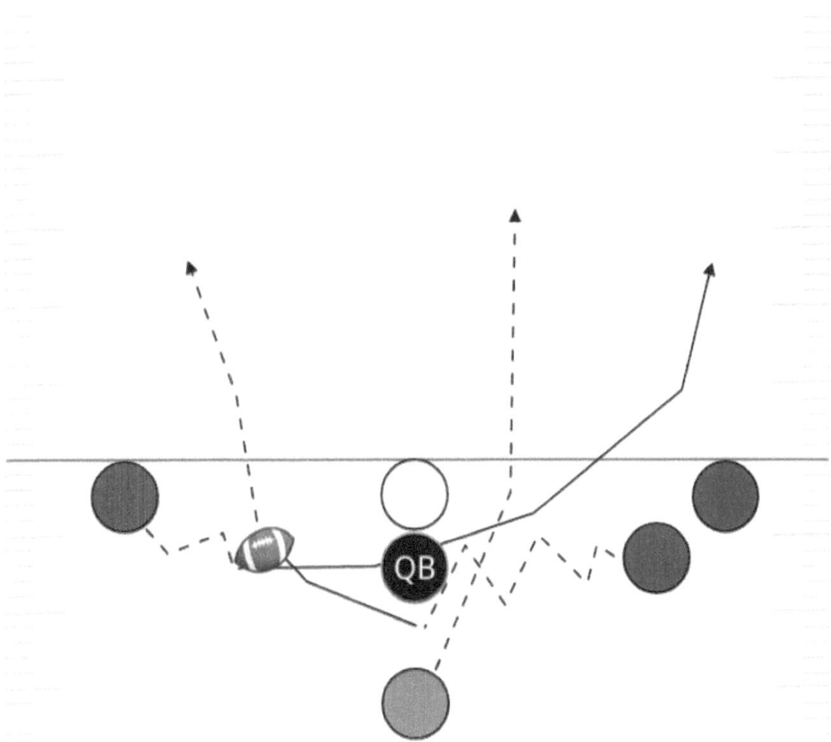

Twins Right, Jet Sweep Reverse
Slot receiver motions toward QB
QB hand off to slot receiver
Running back fakes right
Slot receiver hands off to left receiver

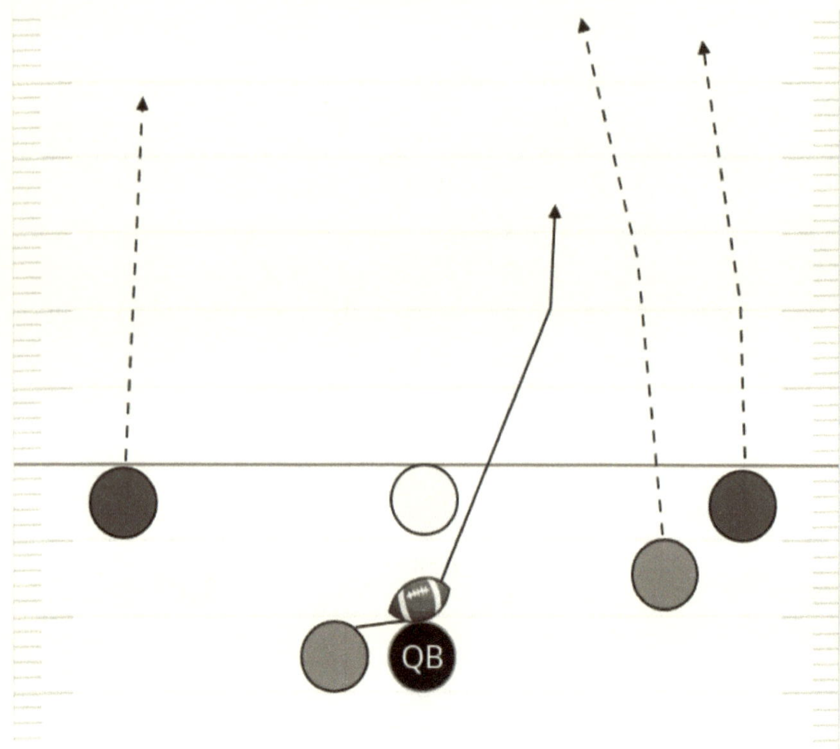

Gun Right, Dive

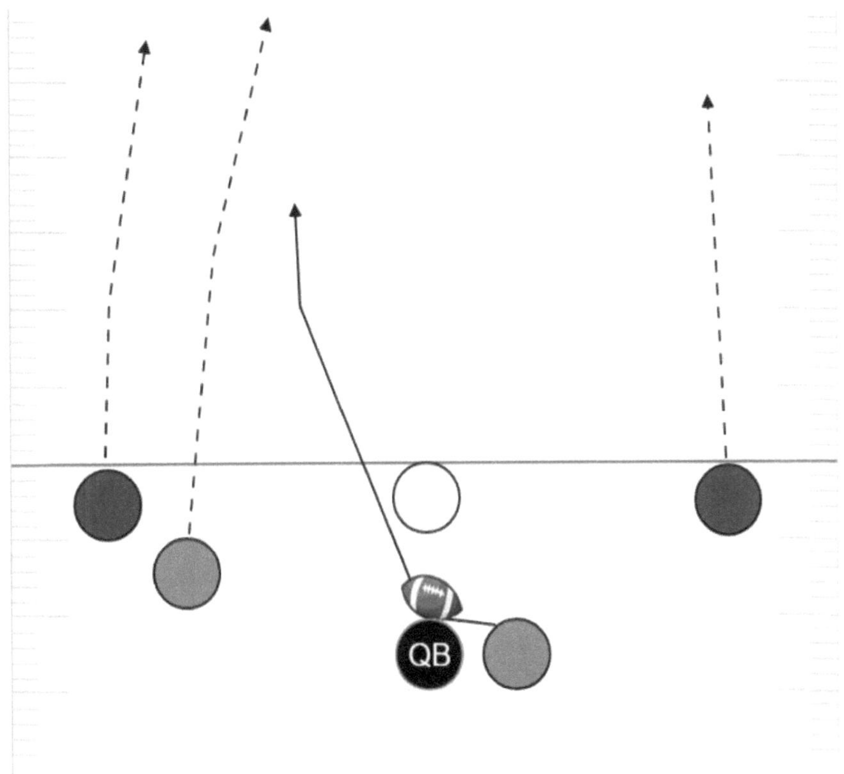

Gun Left, Dive

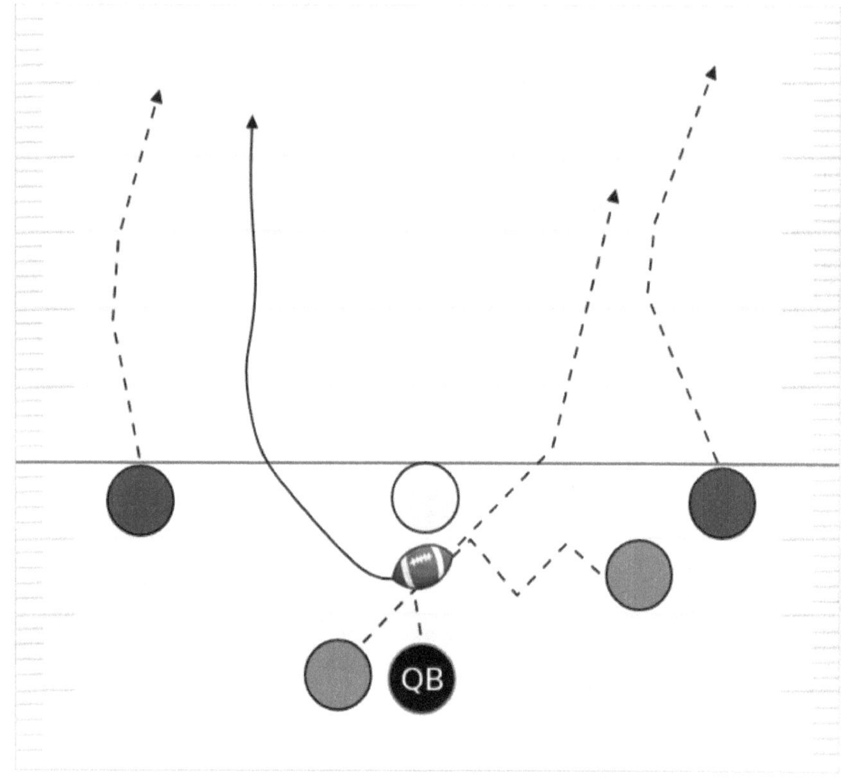

Gun Right, Jet Sweep
Slot receiver motions toward QB
QB shovel passes the ball to slot receiver
Running back fakes right

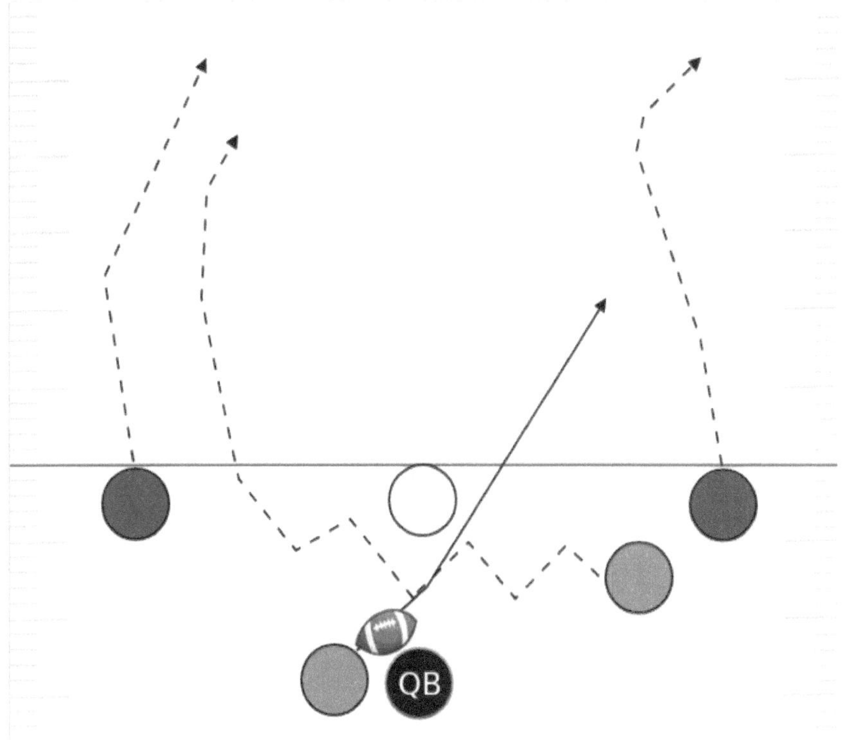

Gun Right, Jet Sweep Counter
Slot receiver motions toward QB
QB fakes the ball to slot receiver
Running back goes right, receives hand off

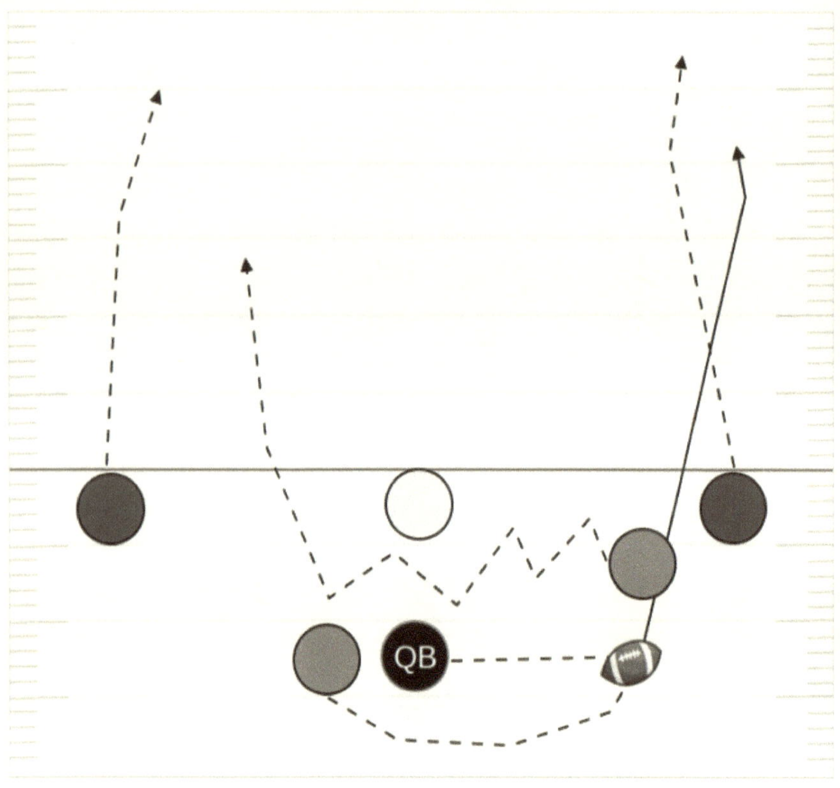

Gun Right, Jet Sweep Counter, Pitch
Slot receiver motions toward QB
QB fakes the ball to slot receiver, fakes hand off to Running back
Running back loops right, QB pitches Running back

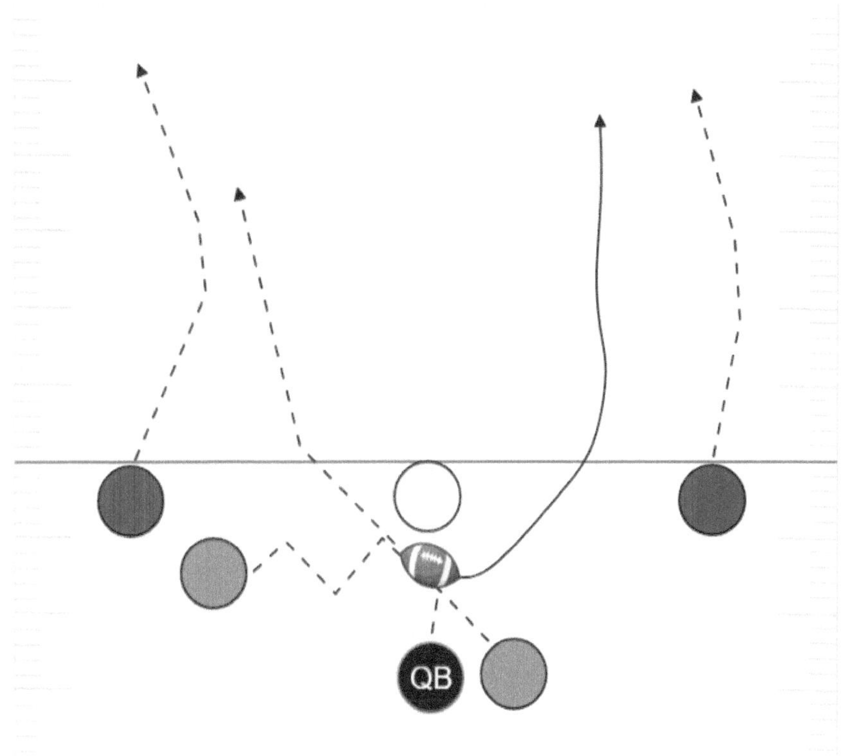

Gun Left, Jet Sweep
Slot receiver motions toward QB
QB shovel passes the ball to slot receiver
Running back fakes left

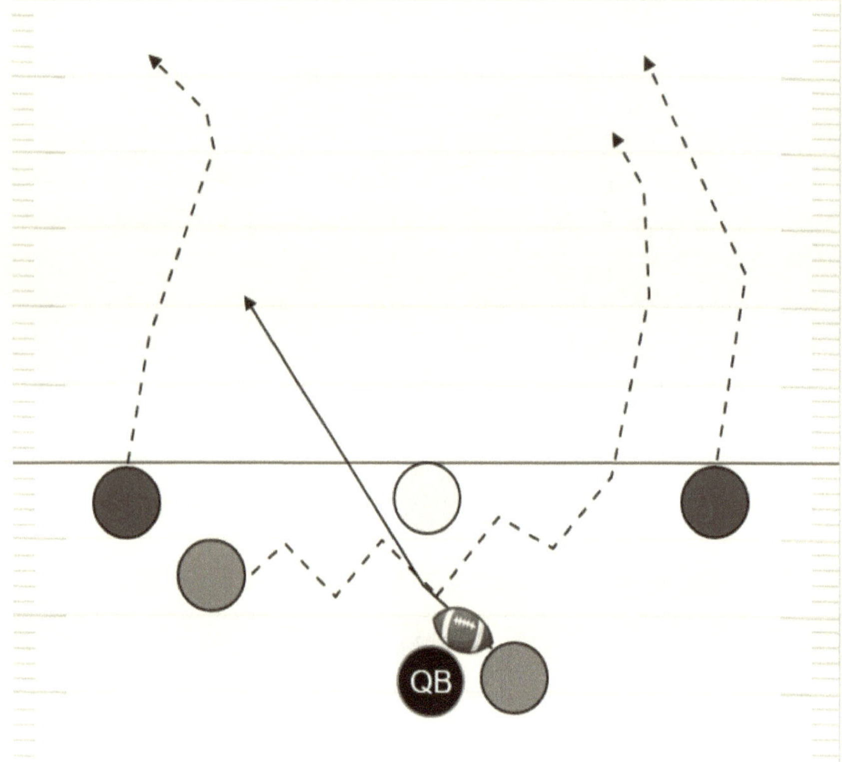

Gun Left, Jet Sweep Counter
Slot receiver motions toward QB
QB fakes the ball to slot receiver
Running back goes left, receives hand off

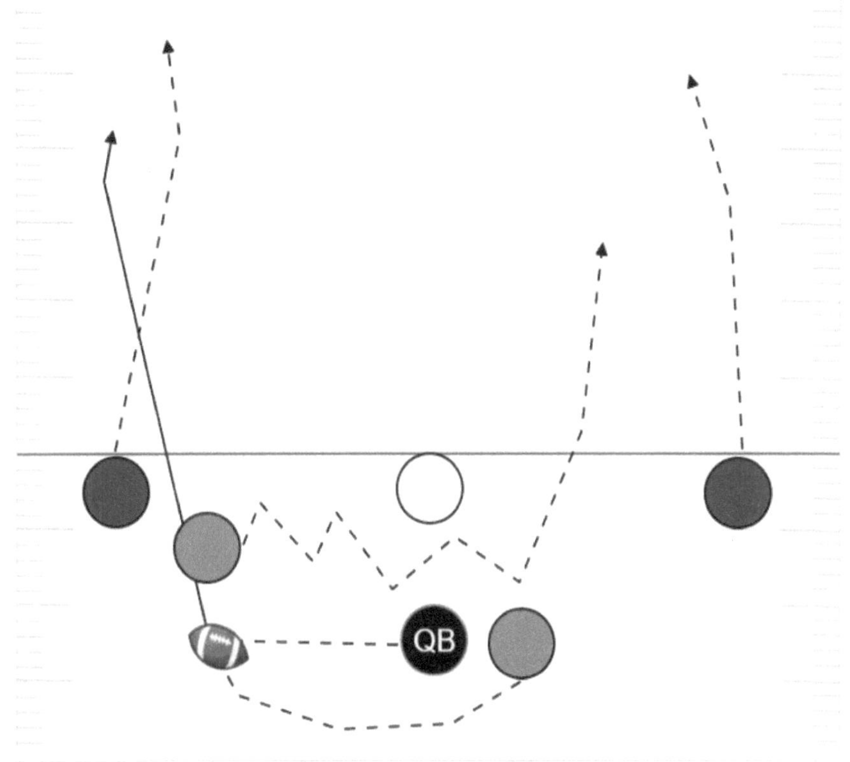

Gun Left, Jet Sweep Counter, Pitch
Slot receiver motions toward QB
QB fakes the ball to slot receiver, fakes hand off to Running back
Running back loops right, QB pitches Running back

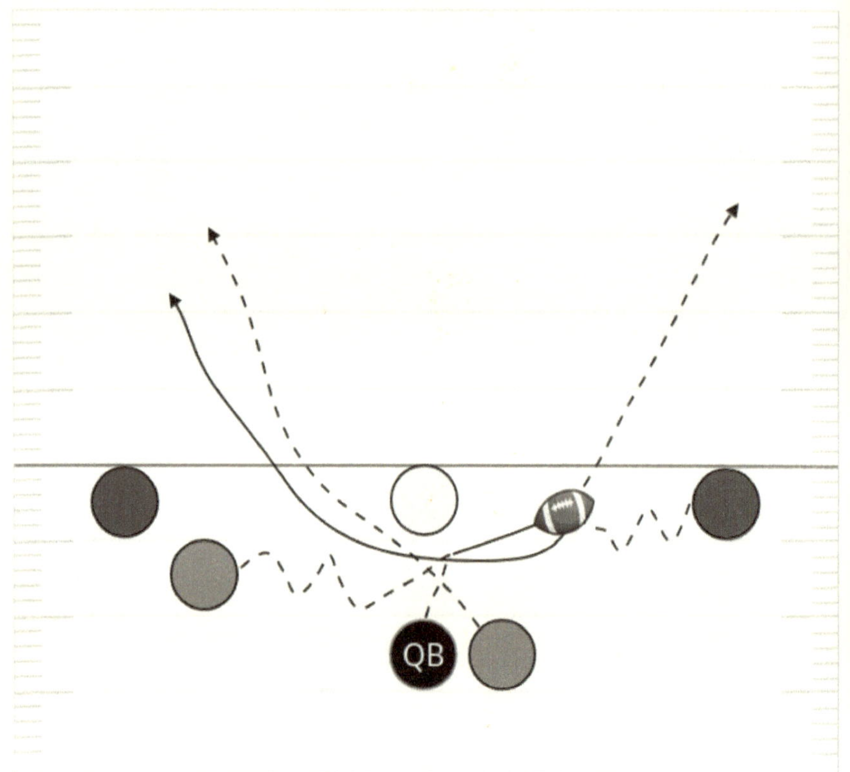

Gun Left, Jet Sweep Reverse
Slot receiver motions toward QB
Running back fakes left
QB shovel passes the ball to slot receiver
Slot receiver hands off to right receiver

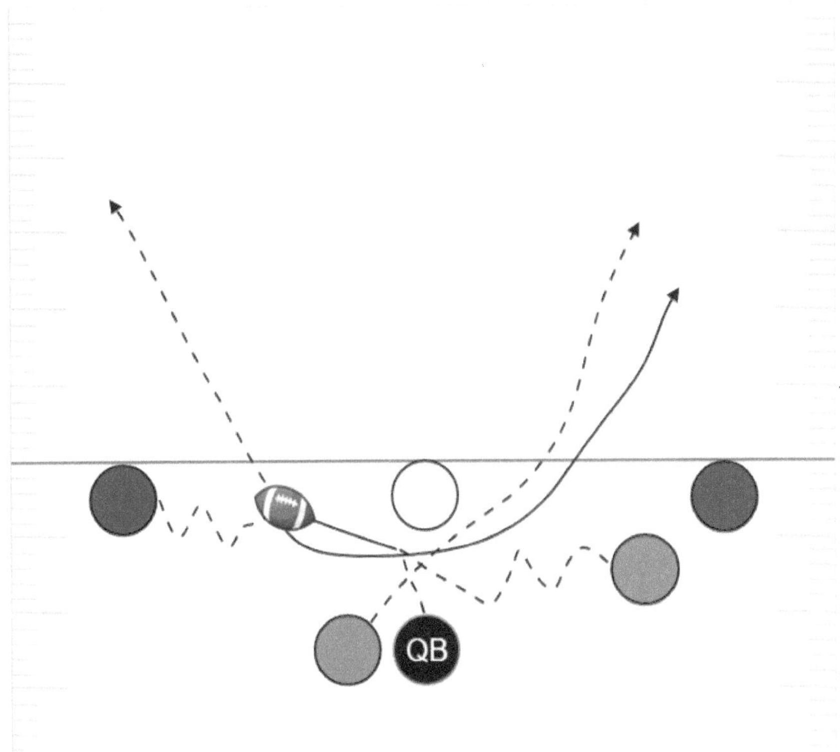

Gun Right, Jet Sweep Reverse
Slot receiver motions toward QB
Running back fakes right
QB shovel passes the ball to slot receiver
Slot receiver hands off to Left receiver

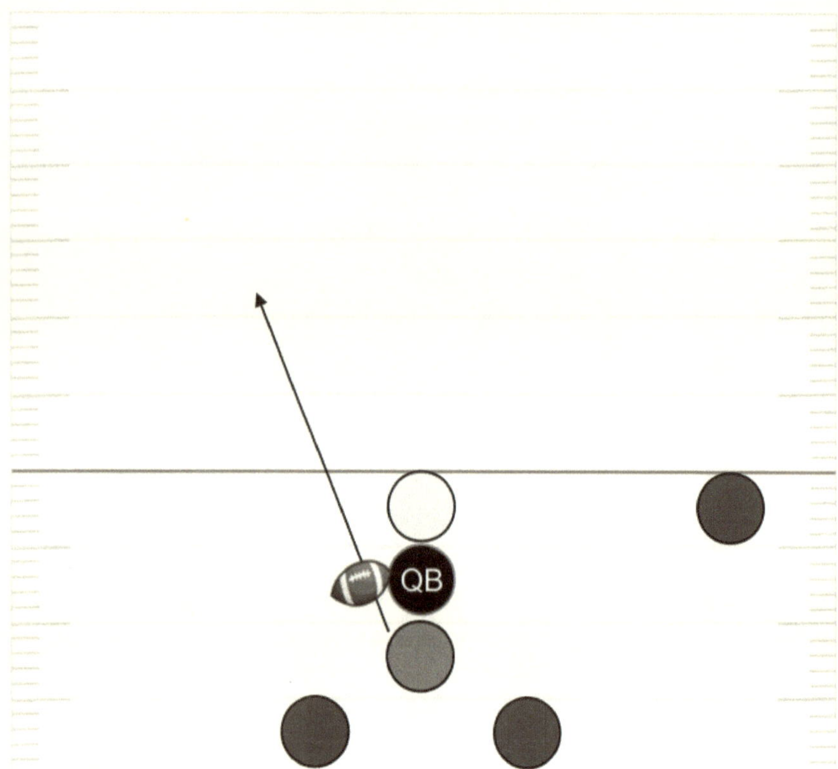

Wishbone Right, Dive Left

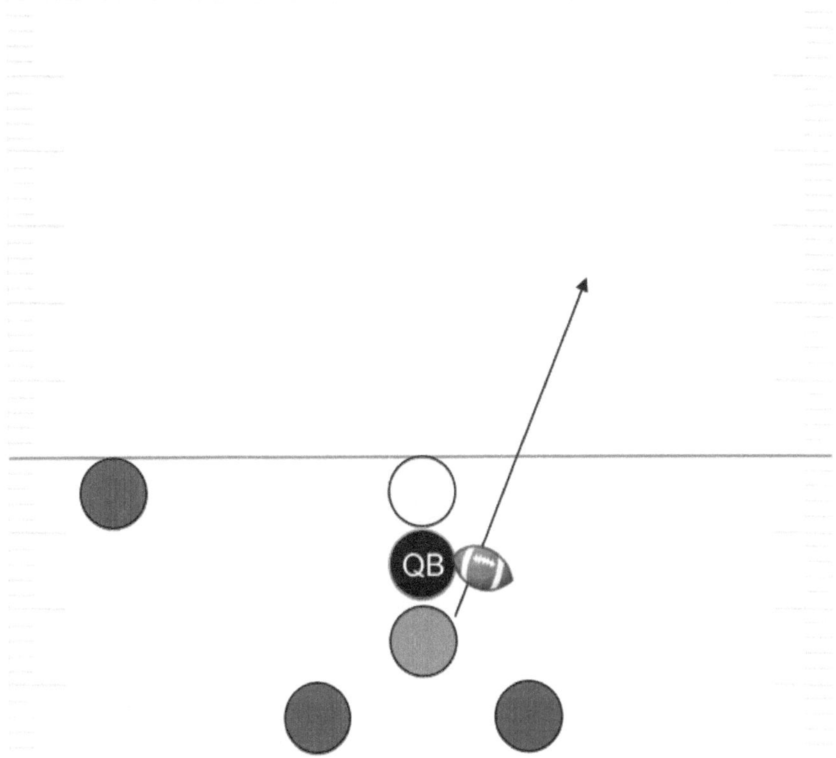

Wishbone Left, Dive Right

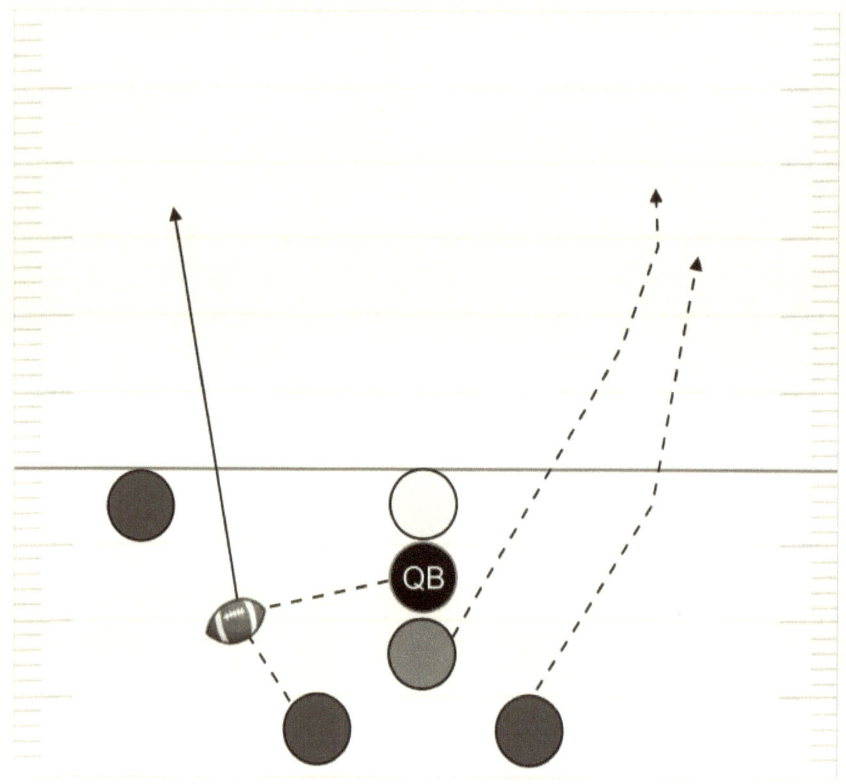

Wishbone Left, Pitch Left

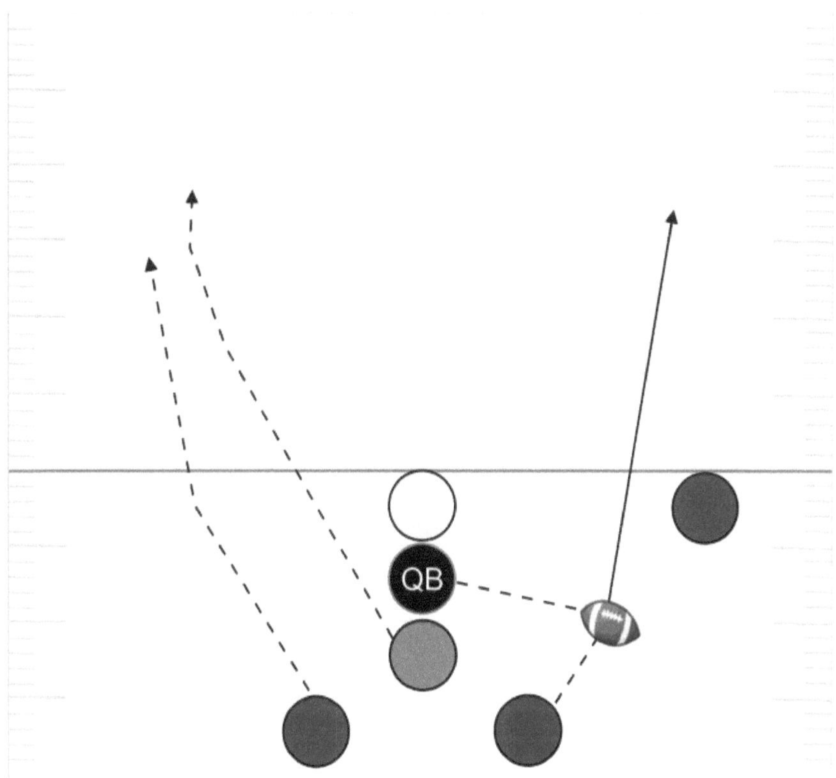

Wishbone Right, Pitch Right

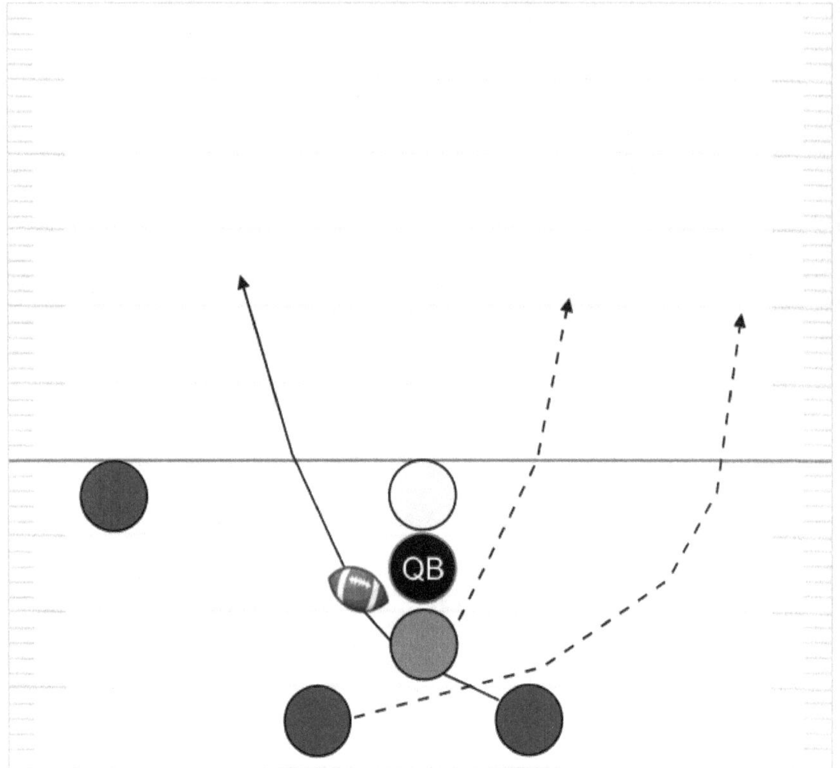

Wishbone Left, Counter Left
QB fakes dive Right
Right back takes handoff
Left back fakes left

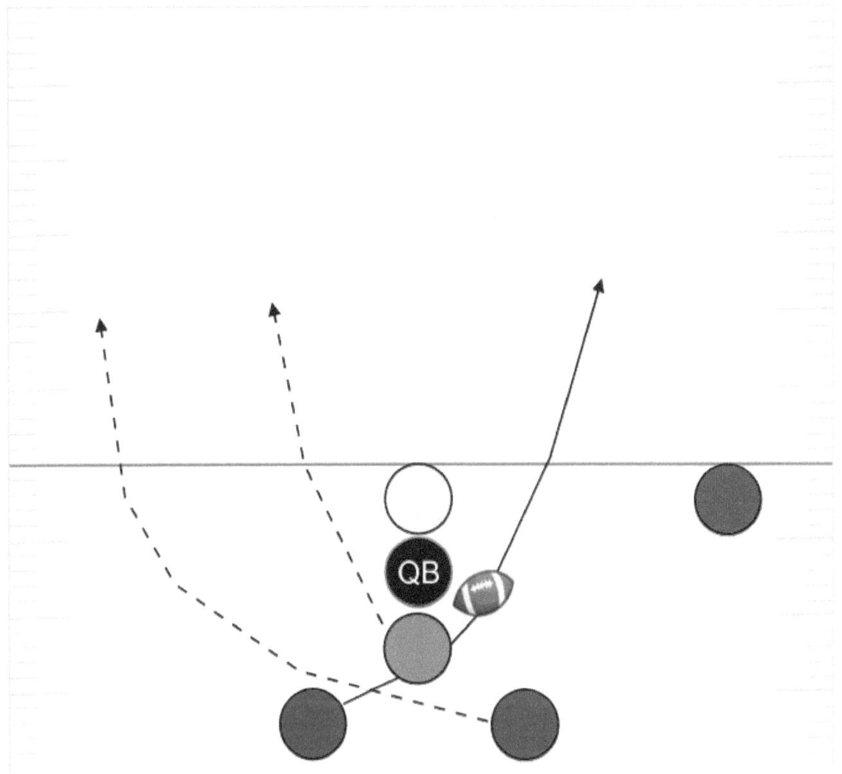

Wishbone Right, Counter Right
QB fakes dive left
Left back takes handoff
Right back fakes left

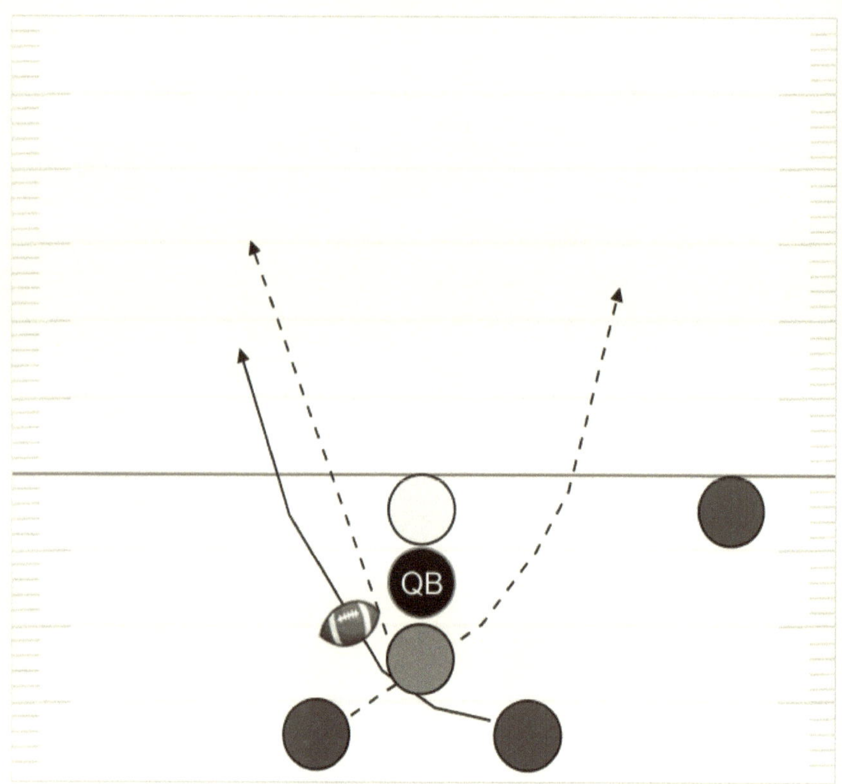

Wishbone Right, Cross Left
QB fakes dive left
Left back fakes handoff
Right back receives handoff

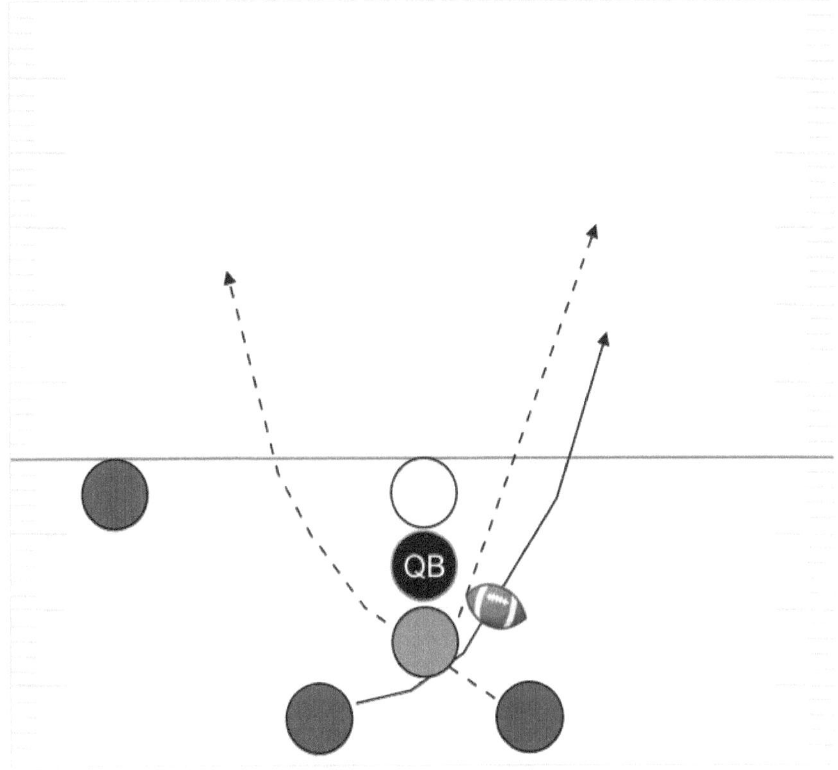

Wishbone Left, Cross Right
QB fakes dive right
Right back fakes handoff
Left back receives handoff

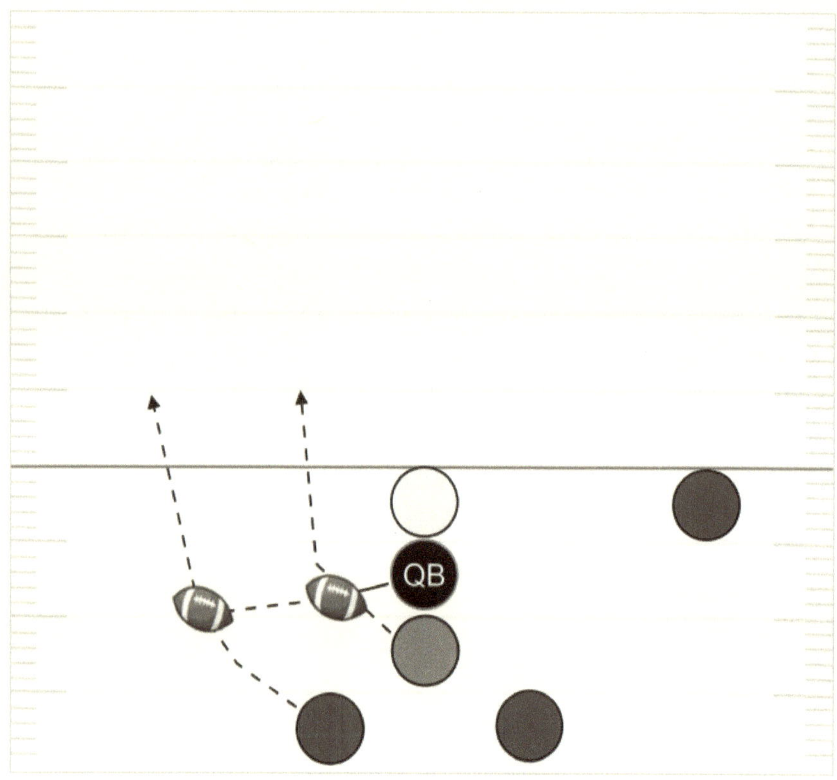

Wishbone Right, Option Left
QB Reads Defense prior to snap
If large gap in middle, give to fullback
If full back is covered by man on center or offset left of center, then pitch to right tailback

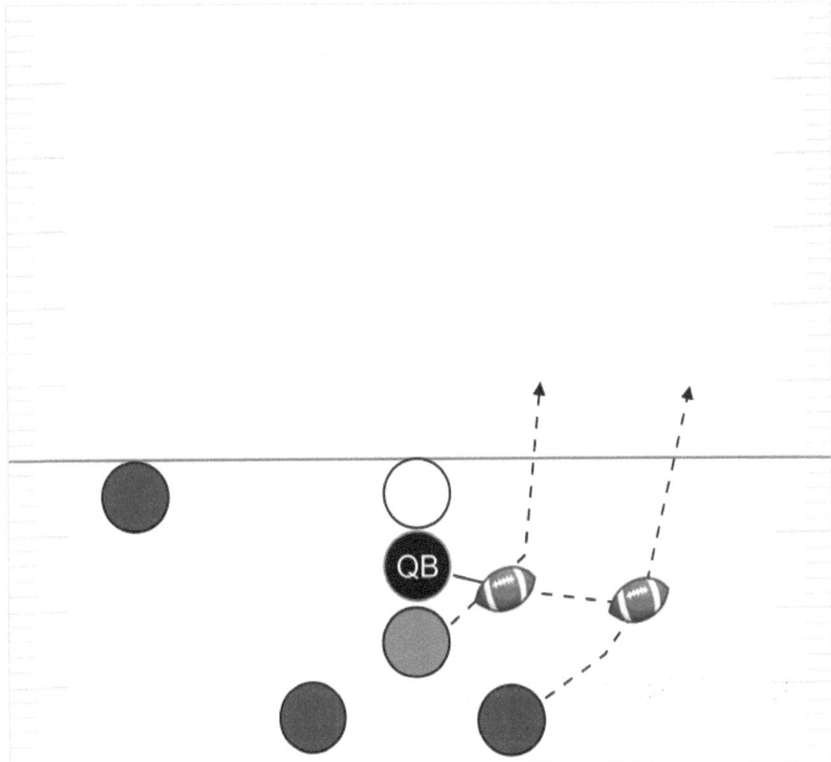

Wishbone Left, Option Right
QB Reads Defense prior to snap
If large gap in middle, give to fullback
If full back is covered by man on center or offset right of center, then pitch to right tailback

PASS PLAYS

62

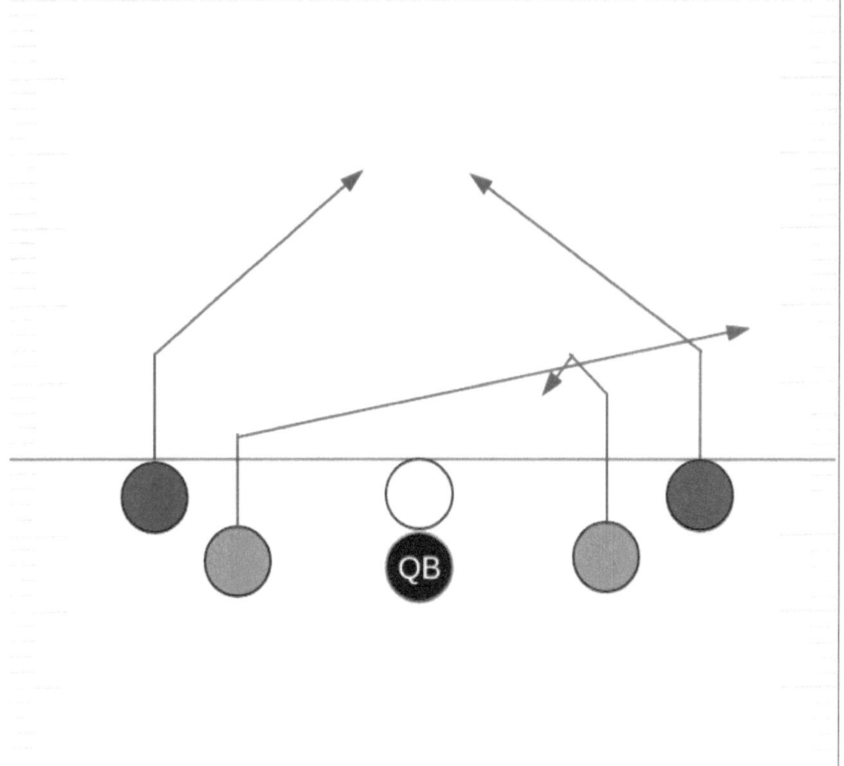

Quads Sample Pass Play
Quads, 8-2-4-8
Pass patterns are left to right

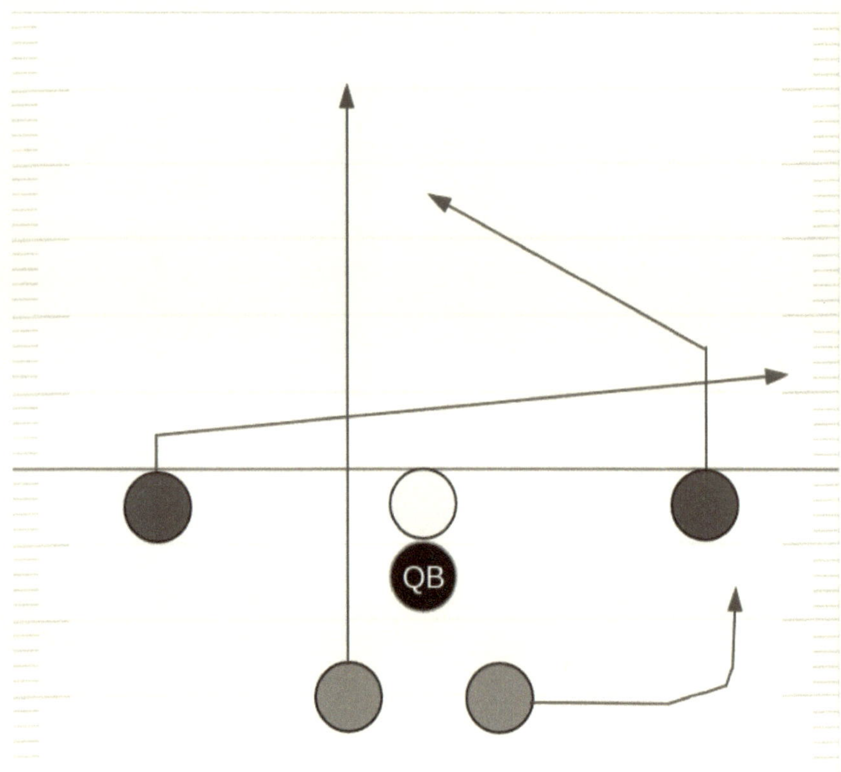

Split Back Sample Pass Play
Split Back, 2-9-1-8
Pass patterns are left to right

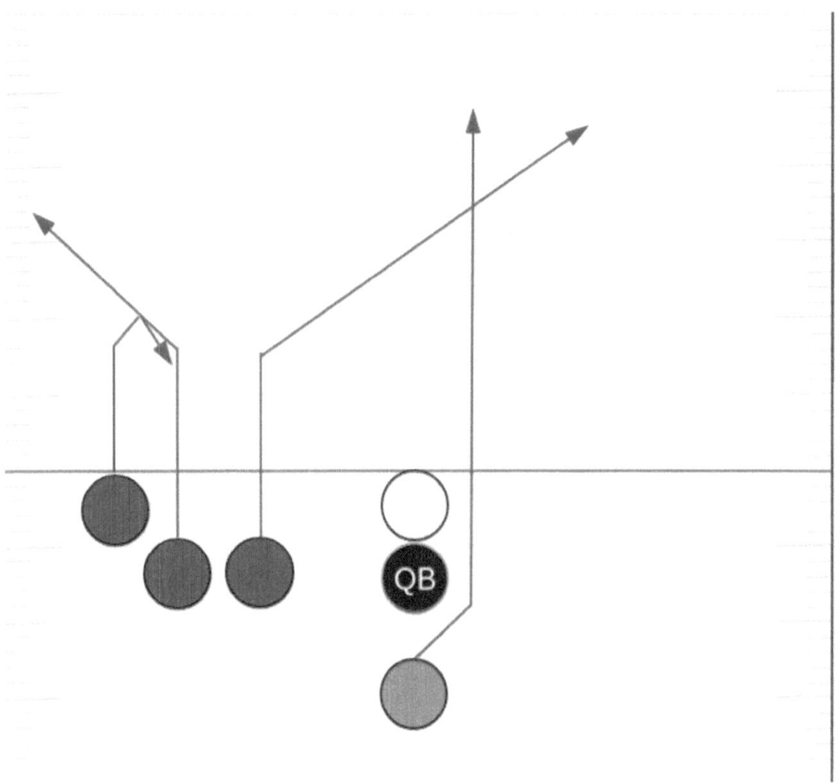

Trips Left Sample Pass Play
Trips Left, 4-7-8-9
Pass patterns are left to right

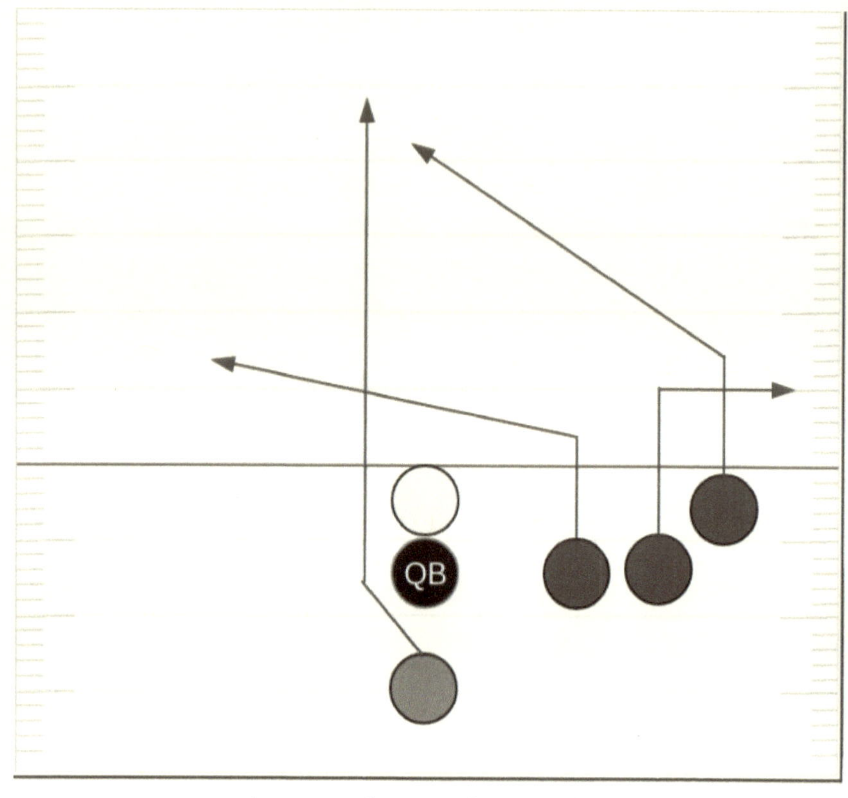

Trips Right Sample Pass Play
Trips Right, 9-2-3-8
Pass patterns are left to right

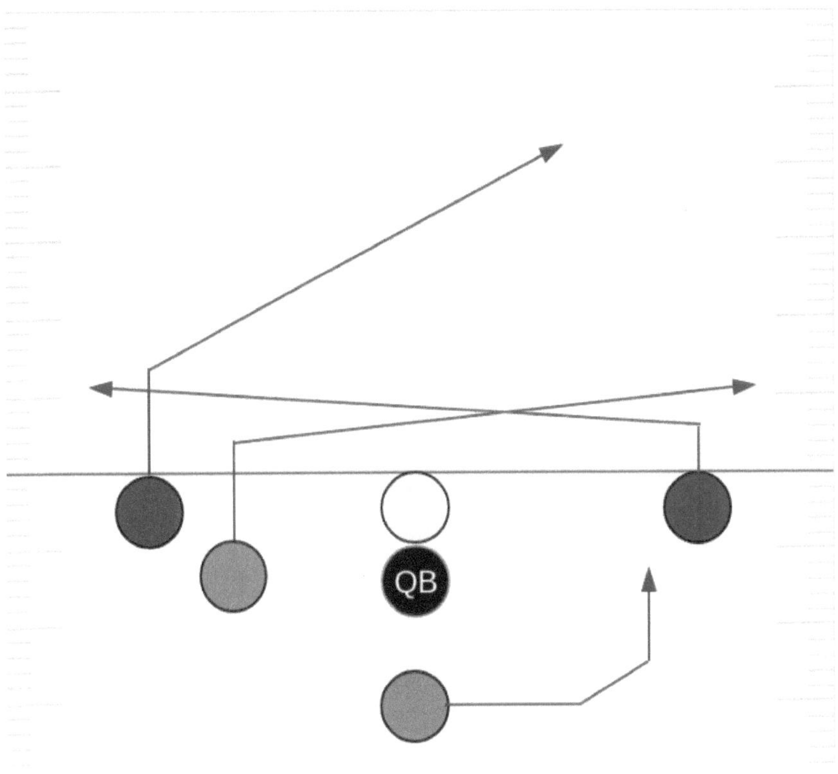

Twins Left Sample Pass Play
Twins Left, 8-2-1-2
Pass patterns are left to right

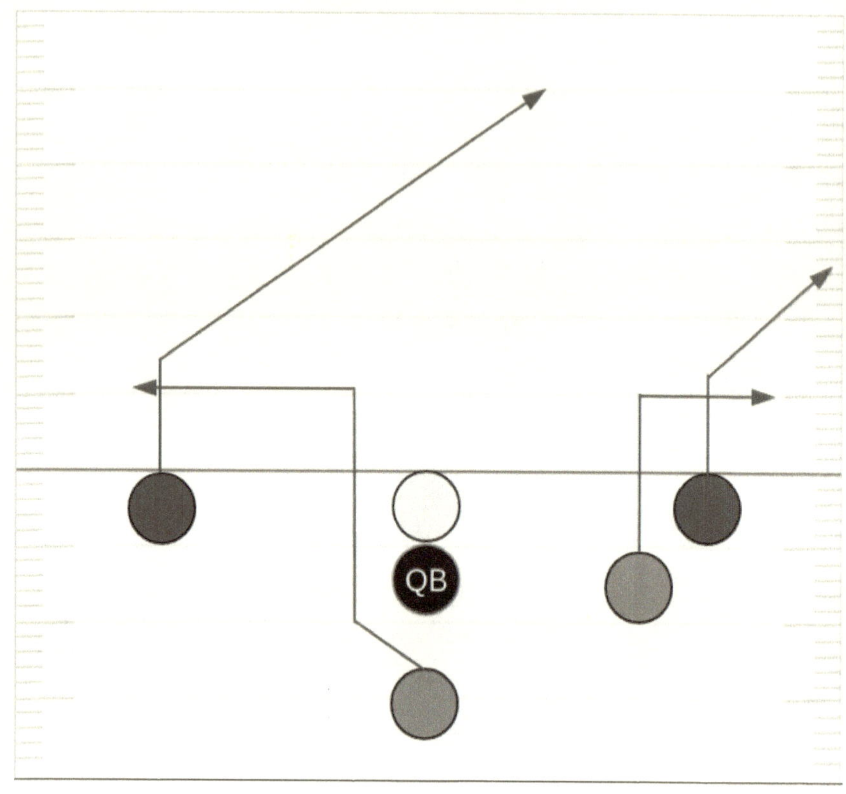

Twins Right Sample Pass Play
Twins Right, 8-3-3-7
Pass patterns are left to right

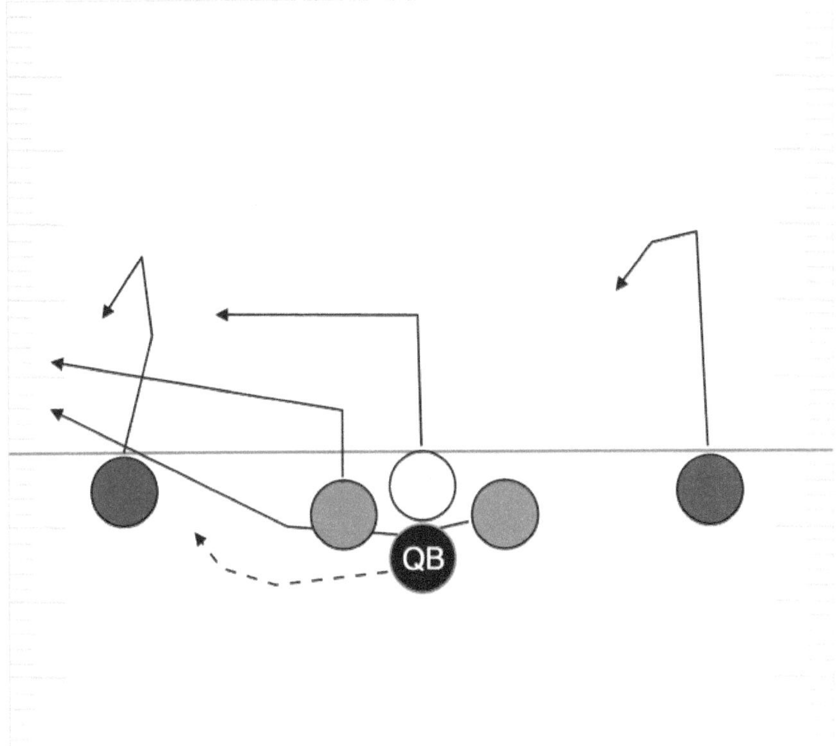

"Zoom" Left
Short yardage, quick pass play
QB rolls left, primary receiver is the slant left.

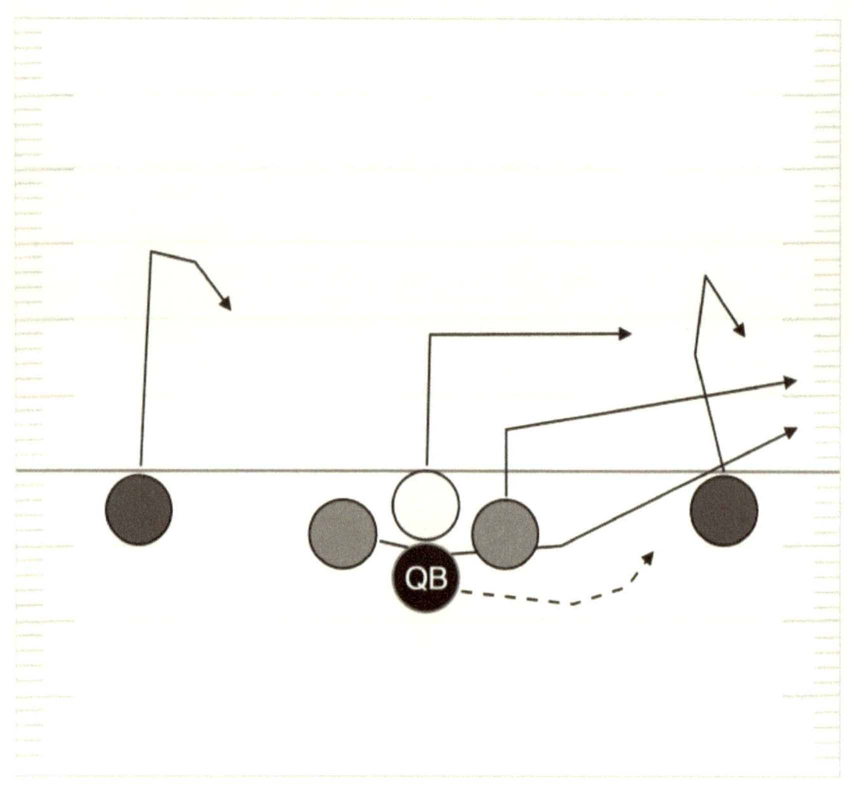

"Zoom" right
Short yardage, quick pass play
QB rolls right, primary receiver is the slant right.

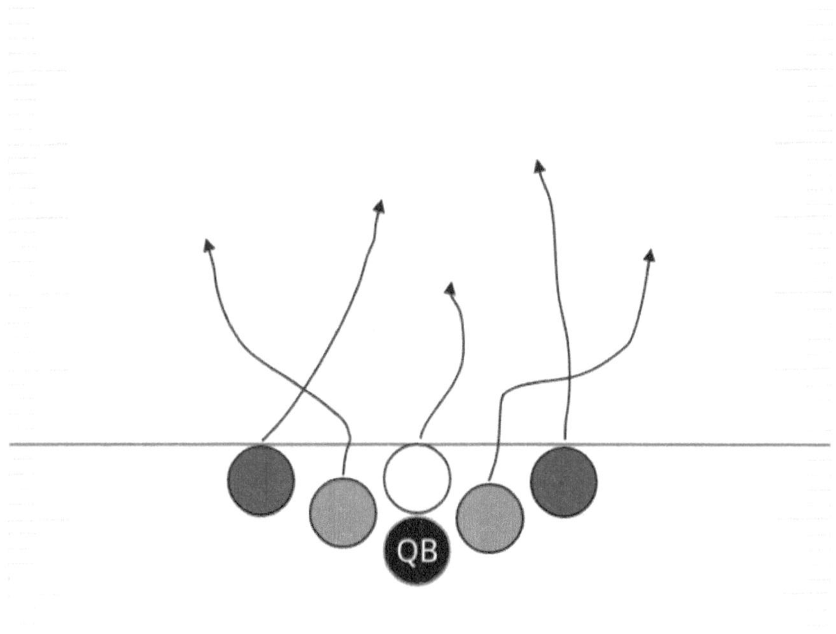

Tight "Fan"
Short yardage, quick pass play
Outside receivers cross with inside receivers
Everyone "fans" out and finds an open spot

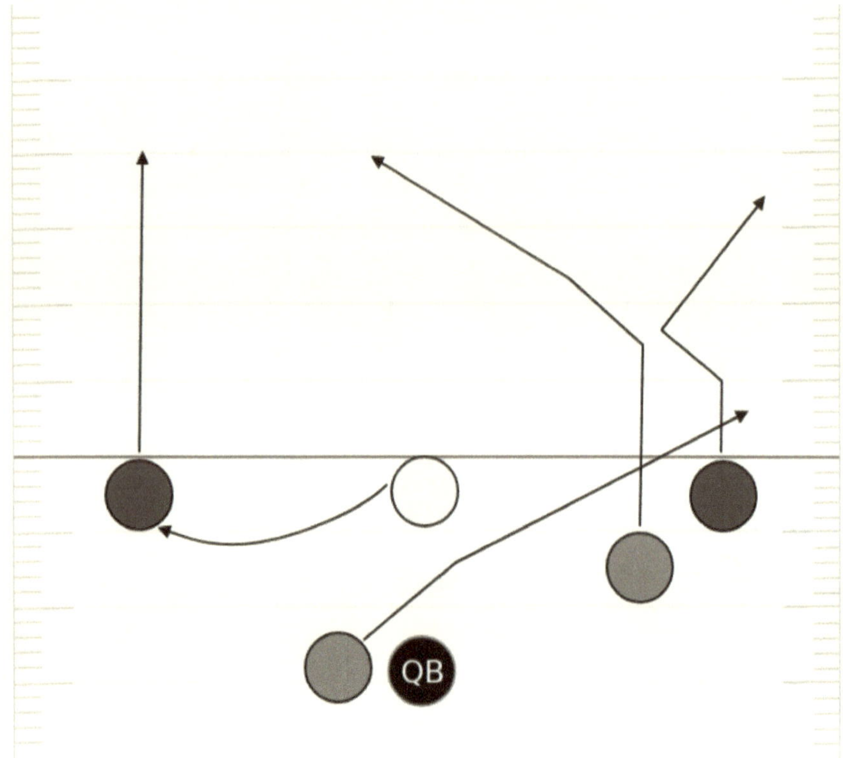

Gun Right Sample Pass Play
Gun Right, Play Action (PA) 9-1-8-Zag
Center loops left
Pass patterns are left to right

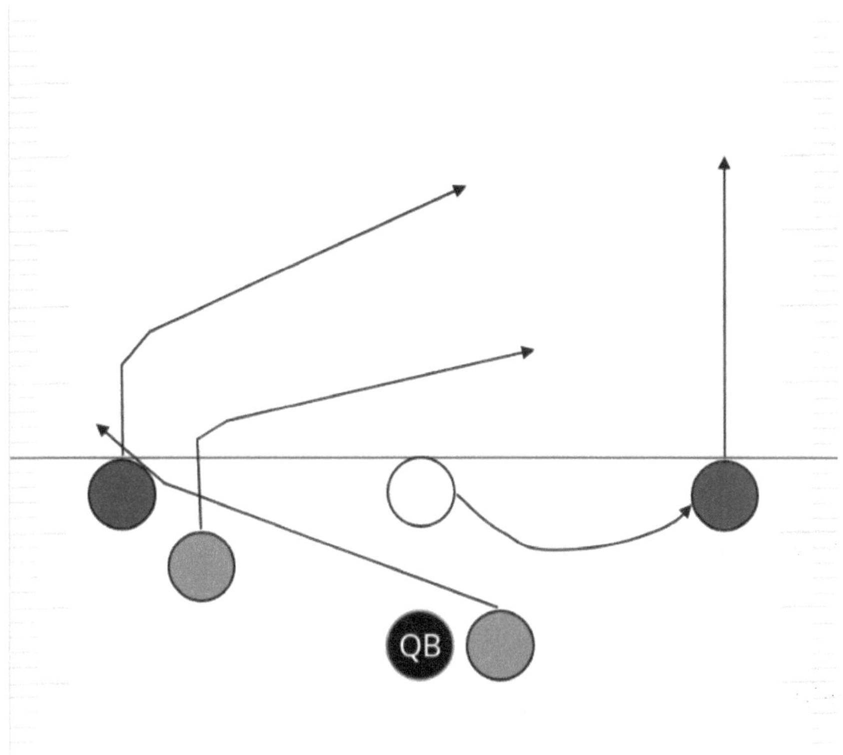

Gun Left Sample Pass Play
Gun Left, Play Action (PA) 8-2-1-9
Center loops left
Pass patterns are left to right

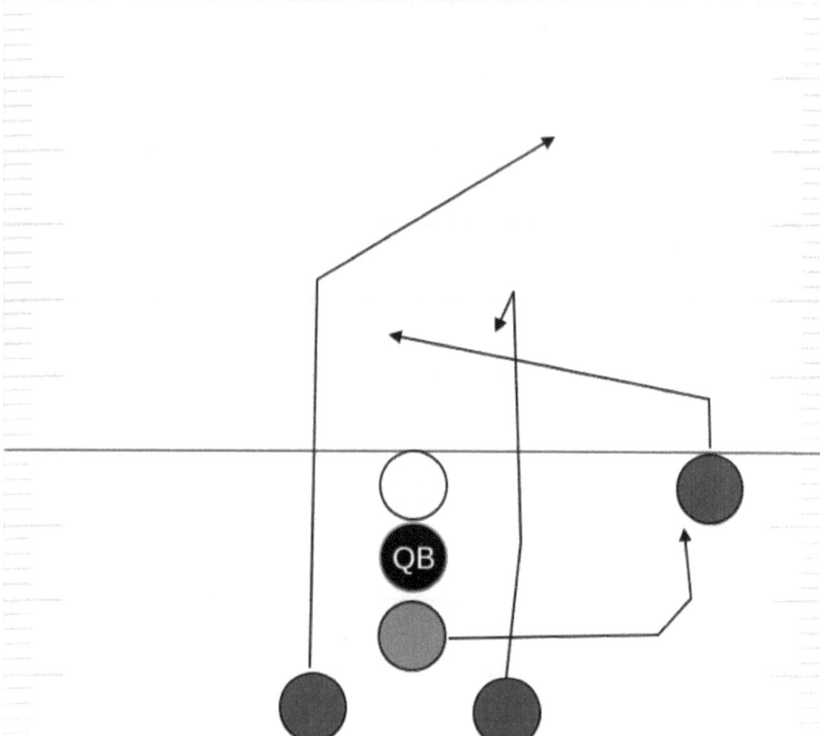

Wishbone Right Sample Pass Play
Wishbone Right, 8-1-4-2
Center loops left
Pass patterns are left to right

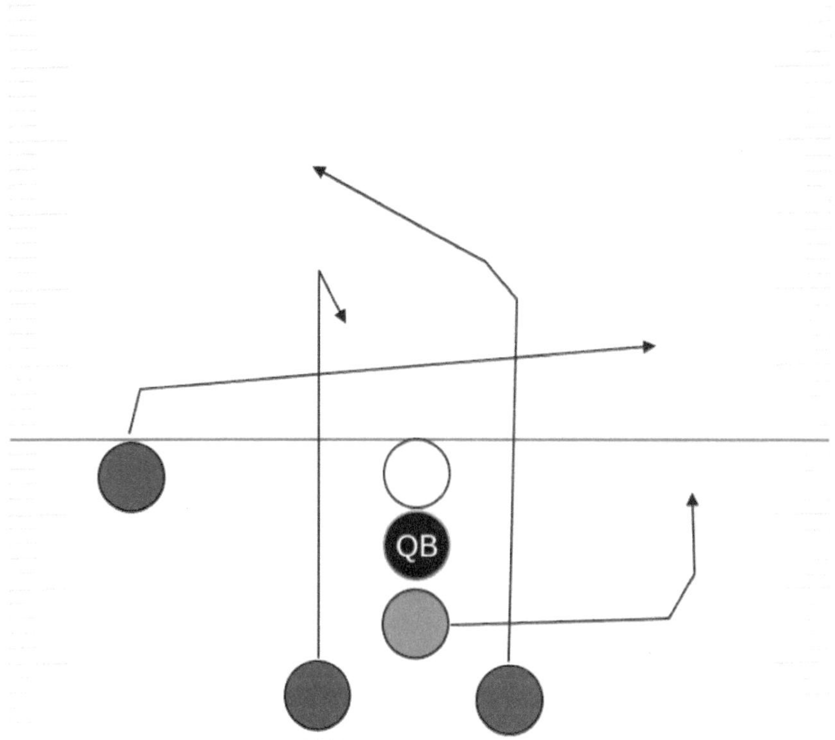

Wishbone Left Sample Pass Play
Wishbone Left, 2-4-1-8

Center loops left
Pass patterns are left to right

DEFENSE

76

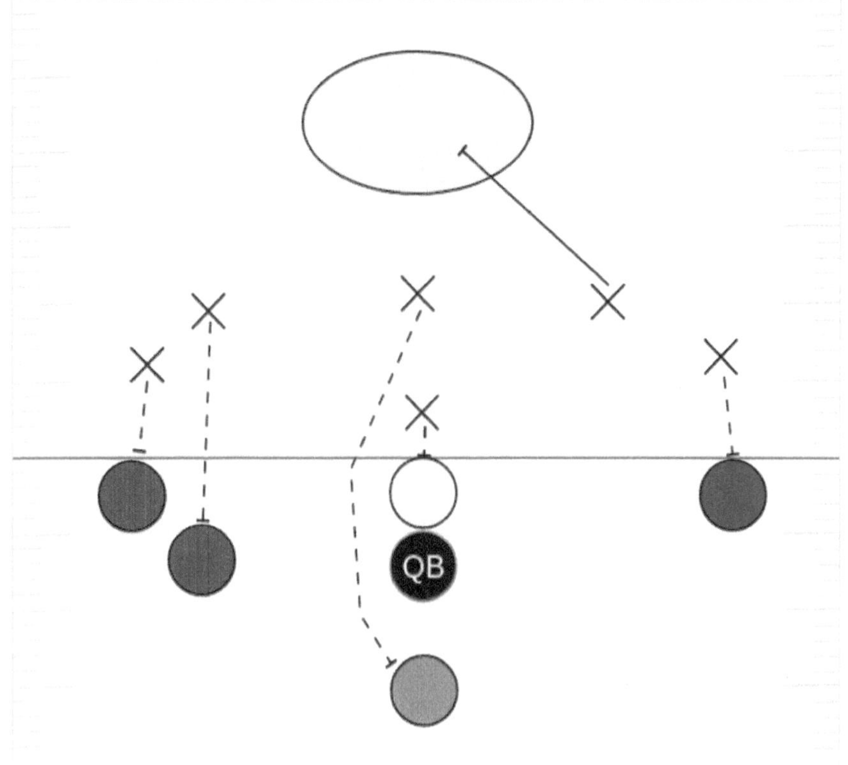

3x3 Man
Each player picks up their main. The free player drops back to a
cover 1, single zone, and mirrors (follows) the QB

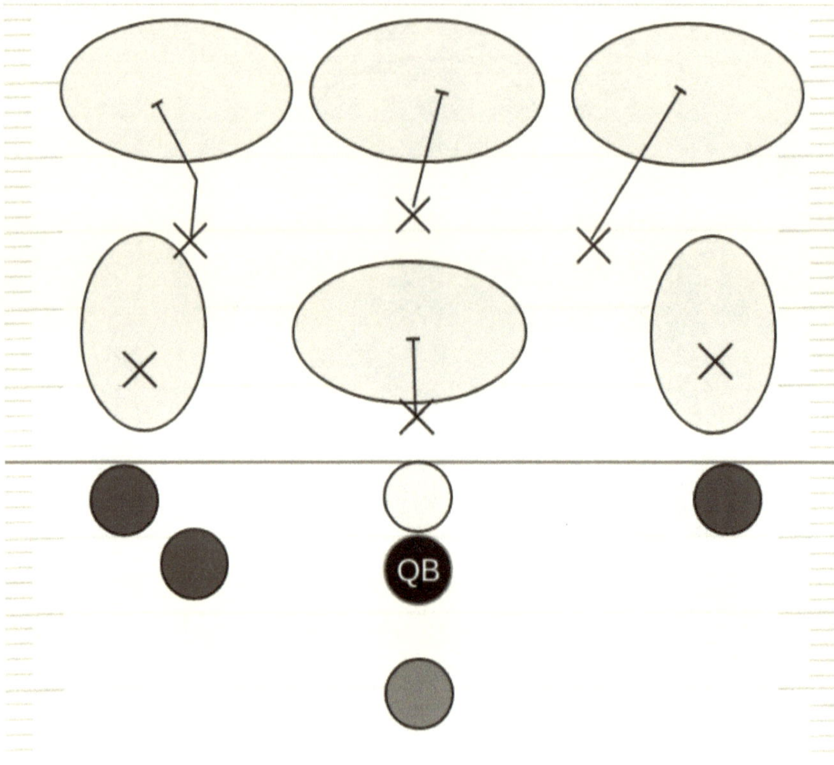

3x3 Zone
Each player covers their designated zone, Linebackers are in cover 3

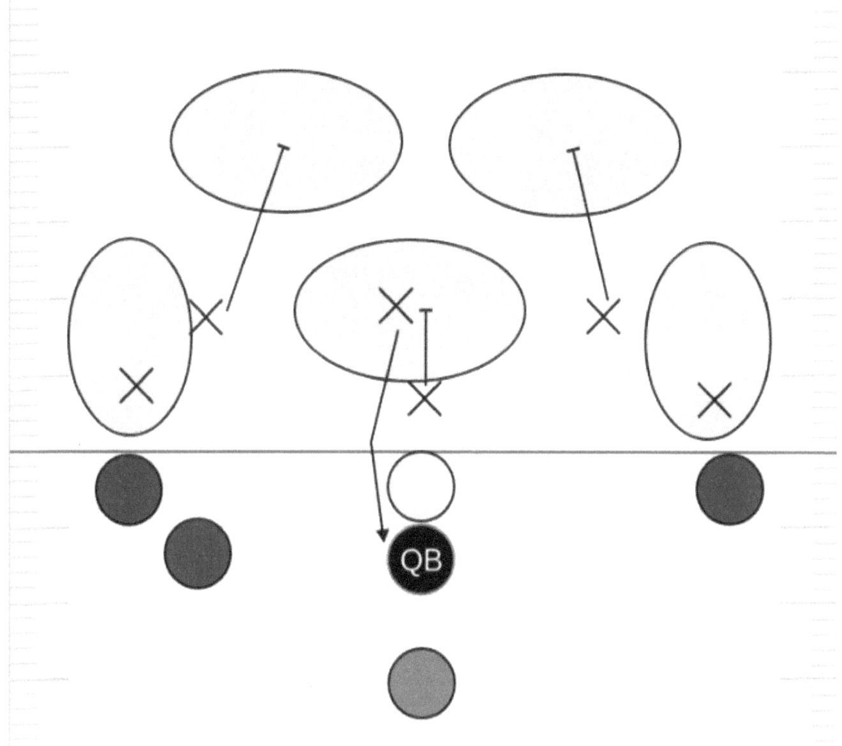

3x3 Zone Blitz
Each player covers their designated zone. Middle defensive back
blitzes QB. Outside Linebackers drop like cover 2 Safeties

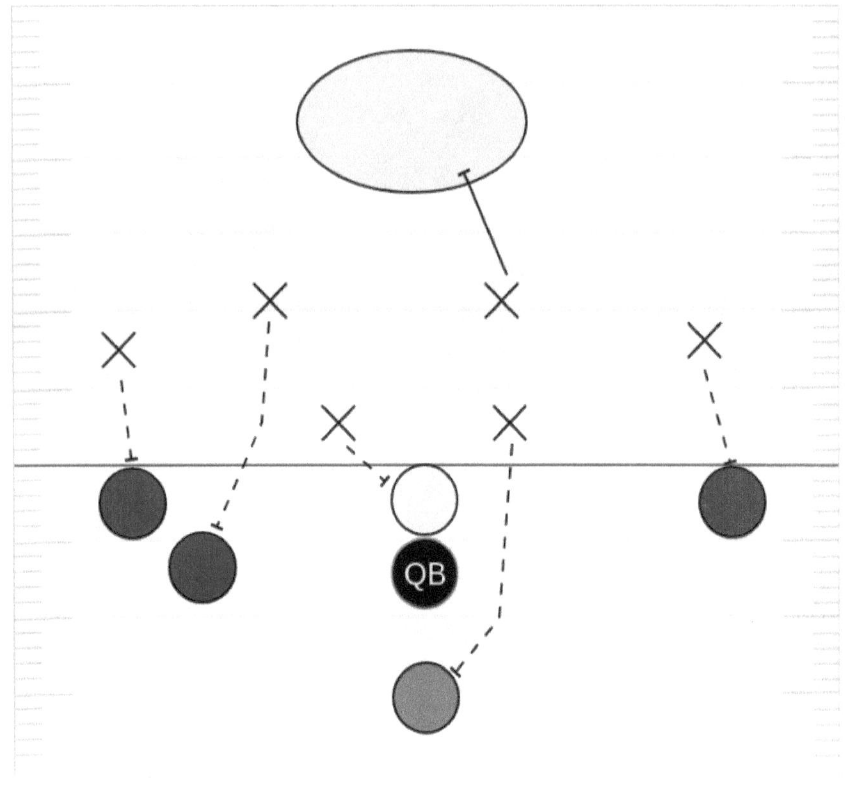

2x4 Man

Each player picks up their main. The free player drops back to a
cover 1, single zone, and mirrors (follows) the QB

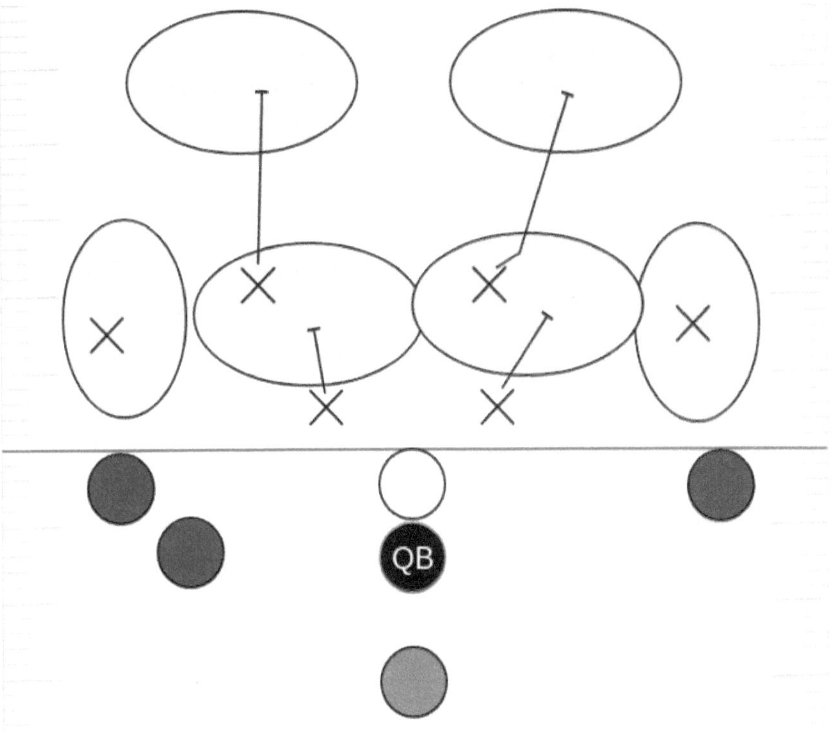

2x4 Zone
Each player covers their designated zone, Inside Linebackers drop
like cover 2 Safeties

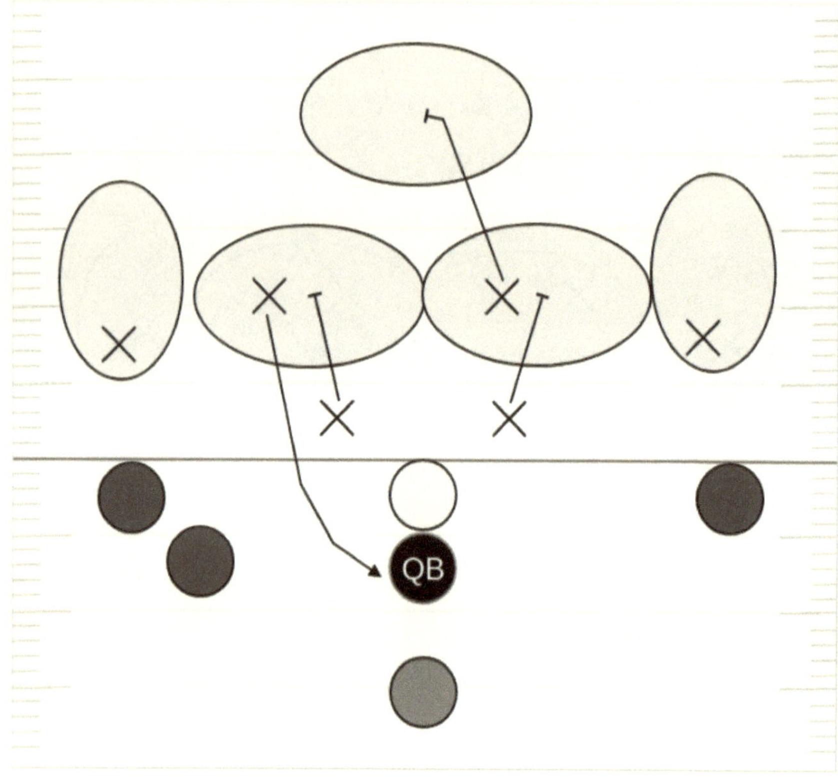

2x4 Zone Blitz
Each player covers their designated zone. Middle backside (the player that the QB would have their back to when passing) defensive back blitzes QB. Remaining inside Linebacker drops to cover 1

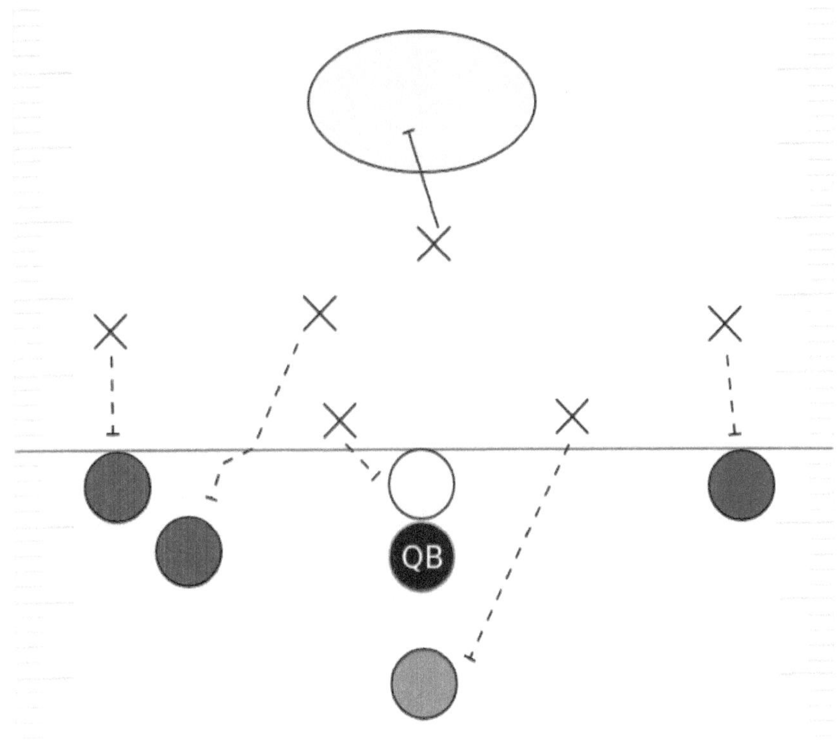

2x3x1 Man

Each player picks up their main. The Safety drops back to a cover 1, single zone, and mirrors (follows) the QB

Similar to 2x4 Man, but we start with a deep Safety

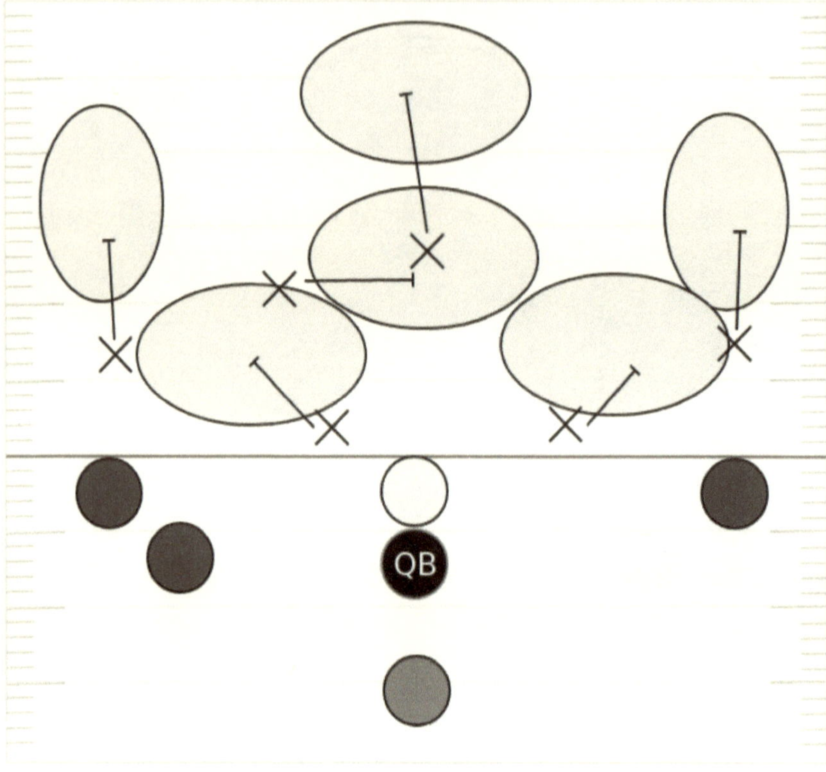

2x3x1 Zone
Each player covers their designated zone. The Safety drops back to a
cover 1, single zone, and mirrors (follows) the QB

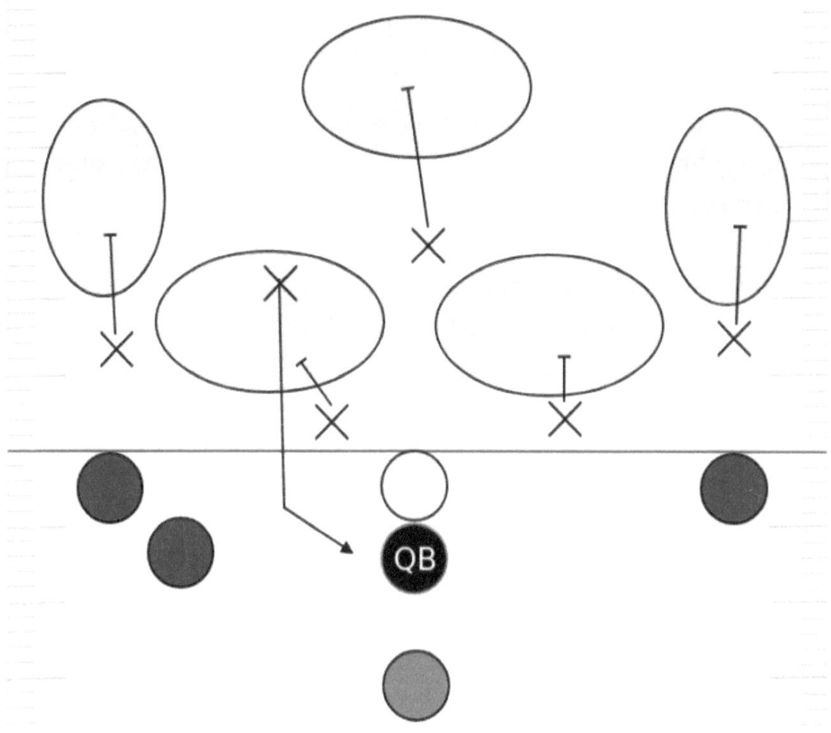

2x3x1 Zone Blitz
Each player covers their designated zone. Middle Linebacker blitzes
QB. The Safety drops back to a cover 1, single zone, and mirrors
(follows) the QB
Similar to 2x4 Man, but we start with a deep Safety

Play Sheet and Wristband

The following is a sample play sheet and the corresponding wristband plays. The coach's play sheet is color coded for common plays, options or counters, deep passes and short yardage. It is organized to have the play first, and then the color call.

The wristbands are organized by color and number that references the play call. It also includes small images of plays and the passing tree to help the kids remember the formations, and plays.

Coach Play Sheet

Formation	Call	Call-Color	Call #	Formation	Call	Call-Color	Call #
Split Backs	Pitch Left	Green	34	Wishbone Left	Counter Left	Red	28
Split Backs	Pitch Right	Green	22	Wishbone Left	Counter Right	Green	21
Gun Twins Left	Dive	Red	38	Wishbone Right	Counter Left	Blue	38
Twins Left	Pitch Left	Red	23	Wishbone Right	Counter Right	Blue	32
Twins Left	Pitch Right	Blue	29	Gun Quads	4 4 4 4	Green	27
Gun Twins Right	Dive	Red	22	Gun Quads	8 2 2 8	Blue	26
Twins Right	Pitch Left	Blue	30	Gun Twins Left	8 2 1 9	Blue	25
Twins Right	Pitch Right	Blue	39	Gun Twins Right	9 1 8 Zag	Red	32
Trips Left	Pitch Left	Blue	36	Quads	4 4 4 4	Blue	33
Trips Left	Pitch Right	Red	24	Quads	8 2 2 8	Green	28
Trips Right	Pitch Left	Blue	24	Split Backs	2 9 1 8	Green	31
Trips Right	Pitch Right	Red	29	Split Backs	4 4 4 4	Green	26
Wishbone Left	Option Left	Blue	22	Tight		Red	21
Wishbone Left	Option Right	Red	25	Trips Left	2 2 2 1	Red	34
Wishbone Right	Option Left	Blue	34	Trips Left	8 6 2 1	Blue	21
Wishbone Right	Option Right	Red	37	Trips Right	1 2 6 8	Green	25
Split Backs	Cross Left	Red	31	Twins Left	8 2 1 2	Green	33
Split Backs	Cross Right	Red	20	Twins Right	2 1 6 4	Blue	35
Twins Left	Jet Sweep	Red	27	Twins Right	6 1 2 9	Red	36
Twins Left	Jet Sweep Counter	Green	30	Twins Right	9 1 2 8	Blue	28
Twins Left	Jet Sweep Reverse	Blue	37	Wishbone Left	2 4 1 8	Red	33
Twins Right	Jet Sweep	Blue	31	Wishbone Right	8 1 3 2	Red	30
Twins Right	Jet Sweep Counter	Red	35	Quads	Shuffle Pass	Green	29
Twins Right	Jet Sweep Reverse	Red	26	Trips Left	Shuffle Pass	Green	23
Wishbone Left	Cross Left	Green	32	Trips Right	Shuffle Pass	Blue	27
Wishbone Left	Cross Right	Blue	23	Zoom	Right	Red	39
Wishbone Right	Cross Left	Blue	20	Zoom	Left	Green	24
Wishbone Right	Cross Right	Green	20				

RED

#	Formation	Call	#	Formation	Call	
20	Split Backs	Cross Right	30	Wishbone Right	8132	Jet Sweep Counter
21	Tight		31	Split Backs	Cross Left	
22	Gun Twins Right	Dive	32	Gun Twins Right	918 Zag	
23	Twins Left	Pitch Left	33	Wishbone Left	2418	
24	Trips Left	Pitch Right	34	Trips Left	2221	Jet Sweep Reverse
25	Wishbone Left	Option Right	35	Twins Right	Jet Sweep Counter	
26	Twins Right	Jet Sweep Reverse	36	Twins Right	6129	
27	Twins Left	Jet Sweep	37	Wishbone Right	Option Right	
28	Wishbone Left	Counter Left	38	Gun Twins Left	Dive	
29	Trips Right	Pitch Right	39	Zoom	Right	

BLUE

#	Formation	Call	#	Formation	Call	
20	Wishbone Right	Cross Left	30	Twins Right	Pitch Left	Wishbone Counter Left
21	Trips Left	8621	31	Twins Right	Jet Sweep	
22	Wishbone Left	Option Left	32	Wishbone Right	Counter Right	
23	Wishbone Left	Cross Right	33	Quads	4444	
24	Trips Right	Pitch Left	34	Wishbone Right	Option Left	Wishbone Cross Right
25	Gun Twins Left	8219	35	Twins Right	2164	
26	Gun Quads	8228	36	Trips Left	Pitch Left	
27	Trips Right	Shuffle Pass	37	Twins Left	Jet Sweep Reverse	
28	Twins Right	9128	38	Wishbone Right	Counter Left	
29	Twins Left	Pitch Right	39	Twins Right	Pitch Right	

GREEN

#	Formation	Call	#	Formation	Call	
20	Wishbone Right	Cross Right	30	Twins Left	Jet Sweep Counter	Zoom Left
21	Wishbone Left	Counter Right	31	Split Backs	2918	
22	Split Backs	Pitch Right	32	Wishbone Left	Cross Left	
23	Trips Left	Shuffle Pass	33	Twins Left	8212	
24	Zoom	Left	34	Split Backs	Pitch Left	Tight
25	Trips Right	1268	35			
26	Split Backs	4444	36			
27	Gun Quads	4444	37			
28	Quads	8228	38			
29	Quads	Shuffle Pass	39			

RED

#	Formation	Call	#	Formation	Call	
20	Split Backs	Cross Right	30	Wishbone Right	8132	Jet Sweep Counter
21	Tight		31	Split Backs	Cross Left	
22	Gun Twins Right	Dive	32	Gun Twins Right	918 Zag	
23	Twins Left	Pitch Left	33	Wishbone Left	2418	
24	Trips Left	Pitch Right	34	Trips Left	2221	Jet Sweep Reverse
25	Wishbone Left	Option Right	35	Twins Right	Jet Sweep Counter	
26	Twins Right	Jet Sweep Reverse	36	Twins Right	6129	
27	Twins Left	Jet Sweep	37	Wishbone Right	Option Right	
28	Wishbone Left	Counter Left	38	Gun Twins Left	Dive	
29	Trips Right	Pitch Right	39	Zoom	Right	

BLUE

#	Formation	Call	#	Formation	Call	
20	Wishbone Right	Cross Left	30	Twins Right	Pitch Left	Wishbone Counter Left
21	Trips Left	8621	31	Twins Right	Jet Sweep	
22	Wishbone Left	Option Left	32	Wishbone Right	Counter Right	
23	Wishbone Left	Cross Right	33	Quads	4444	
24	Trips Right	Pitch Left	34	Wishbone Right	Option Left	Wishbone Cross Right
25	Gun Twins Left	8219	35	Twins Right	2164	
26	Gun Quads	8228	36	Trips Left	Pitch Left	
27	Trips Right	Shuffle Pass	37	Twins Left	Jet Sweep Reverse	
28	Twins Right	9128	38	Wishbone Right	Counter Left	
29	Twins Left	Pitch Right	39	Twins Right	Pitch Right	

GREEN

#	Formation	Call	#	Formation	Call	
20	Wishbone Right	Cross Right	30	Twins Left	Jet Sweep Counter	Zoom Left
21	Wishbone Left	Counter Right	31	Split Backs	2918	
22	Split Backs	Pitch Right	32	Wishbone Left	Cross Left	
23	Trips Left	Shuffle Pass	33	Twins Left	8212	
24	Zoom	Left	34	Split Backs	Pitch Left	Tight
25	Trips Right	1268	35			
26	Split Backs	4444	36			
27	Gun Quads	4444	37			
28	Quads	8228	38			
29	Quads	Shuffle Pass	39			

About the Author

Jordon Replogle brings a wealth of experience from the gridiron to the pages of his debut book. Born and raised in the heartland of football passion, Jordon's journey through the sport has been nothing short of extraordinary. From his formative years in high school to the intense competition of college football, followed by stints in the semi-pro leagues and even the adrenaline-pumping arena football scene, Replogle's life has been intricately woven with the threads of the game.

Beyond his remarkable playing career, Jordon Replogle has dedicated himself to the art of coaching, contributing eight seasons of his expertise to the world of flag football. His passion for the game extends beyond the field, as he seamlessly transitions from player to mentor, sharing his knowledge and shaping the next generation of football enthusiasts.

Read more at https://www.jordonr.com.